Proper Hotspots in London

I dedicate this book to my
niece Rosa Parker.

Thanks to Giles and Nikki for their
belief, to Nick for his foresight
and Ellie for her inspiration.

Also to my mother, Anjana and to Tom.

Special thanks to John Rai and
Nicola for their research.

Property Hotspots in London

Where in our capital city to buy and let property for profit

Ajay Ahuja

howtobooks

How to Books would like to thank Strategic Rail Authority (SRL), Docklands Light Railway Ltd, Transport for London and Crossrail for their kind permission to reproduce the maps included in this book.

Readers should be aware that any proposed extensions are at present only core proposals and are in need of final sign off by the Department of Transport. Changes may occur during the life of each project.

First published in 2003 by
How To Books Ltd, 3 Newtec Place
Magdalen Road, Oxford OX4 1RE. United Kingdom.
Tel: (01865) 793806. Fax: (01865) 248780.
email: info@howtobooks.co.uk
http://www.howtobooks.co.uk

British Library Cataloguing in Publication Data
A catalogue record for this book is available from the British
Library

Cover design by Baseline Arts Ltd, Oxford
Produced for How To Books by Deer Park Productions
Typeset by Pantek Arts Ltd, Maidstone, Kent
Printed and bound by Bell & Bain Ltd, Glasgow

NOTE: The material contained in this book is set out in good
faith for general guidance and no liability can be accepted
for loss or expense incurred as a result of relying in particular
circumstances on statements made in the book. The laws and
regulations are complex and liable to change, and readers should
check the current position with the relevant authorities before
making personal arrangements.

Contents

A Note From the Author

I started with nothing. I bought my first property when I was 24 with £500 and now I am 30 and I own 60 properties and earn an income in excess of £250,000p.a. It's not difficult but requires DEDICATION, PERSISTENCE and DISCIPLINE. If you lack any of the above then forget it. However, if you have all of the above then welcome. I bought my first property in 1996 for myself to live in. I couldn't get used to it, so I let it out. I soon realised that the tenant was paying my mortgage as well as my beer money (about £120 per month), and required minimal effort from myself. I thought, 'this is easy!', so I bought another one and did the same. Fifty-eight properties later … you get the idea.

My dedication, persistence and discipline I had to becoming rich was not driven by money, but by freedom – the freedom to do what I like, when I like without restriction from my boss or my wallet. Freedom does not have to be your driving factor, it could be a brand new Ferrari or private schooling for your children or simply financial security. Whatever it is, it's this that will keep you going. With the right properties, financial products and tenants, there is no doubt you will succeed. Property has made more millionaires than any other type of business or investment over the last 100 years. This is fact. When you understand property properly it will be obvious that this type of investment is a sure way to long term wealth.

So why choose property? Why not invest in stocks and shares? I'll tell you why. The first reason is that property carries an inherent low risk factor. Houses will not go out of fashion or become obsolete like services or products. They are an essential for us all. That's why house prices have consistently doubled every 10–15 years in the last century. Coupled with the fact that monthly rental values rise with wages (which is a function of inflation) and that the mortgage payment is relatively fixed (only altering with interest rate fluctuations) the profit element always rises. In addition, after the mortgage has been paid, the rent is all profit. That's why many people see investing in property as their pension fund.

The second reason is basic economics. With an expanding population, fragmenting families, an ever moving workforce, fewer properties for sale and fewer council owned properties, THE DEMAND FOR RENTAL PROPERTIES EXCEEDS SUPPLY.

The third reason is an inherent attribute in all of us – we are lazy! To play the stock market properly requires lengthy research, ongoing monitoring and nerves of steel for the duration of the investment. That's why 3 out of 4 private investors lose money. When a property is set up properly, you just sit back and watch the money roll in.

I am a chartered accountant (I left employment when I was 27 to do the property business) and I must admit, the training I received in accountancy and more importantly, in business, has helped me in my success. Through my experience I am able to isolate the key variables in investing in property and present them in this book. No list is ever complete, but these key variables will help you determine which area or areas are right for you. I hope you find this book useful whatever your goals are – this may be to buy a second home to earn a little additional income, or to build a multi-million pound empire.

If you need help in building your property portfolio contact me: Tel: 0800 652 3979; Fax: 01277 362563; 99 Moreton Rd, Ongar, Essex, CM5 0AR or visit my website www.accdirect.co.uk.

How the Book Works

What is a Hotspot?

A hotspot is an area where there are properties available for sale that fall into one of these categories:

Category	Description
A	Property prices are predicted to rise at a greater rate than the national average AND the rental yield is greater than the national average.
B	The rental yield is greater than the national average.
C	Property prices are predicted to rise at a greater rate than the national average.

I have ranked the categories, with category A being the most desirable as it enjoys the best of both worlds – capital growth and yield, thus spreading the return and overall risk. Category B is ranked second as the yield is a definite outcome, whereas capital growth is categorised as C because it is a less certain outcome.

I've found in my experience that investors choose category A, B or C on personal circumstances but more so on gut reaction. My advice is to choose all of them! There is no need to place all your eggs in one basket. Property is a relatively safe investment but there is a degree of uncertainty, so if possible, by investing in all the categories above you eliminate some of the business risk.

Identification of a Hotspot

So how did I identify the hotspots listed? Well the categories are based on two factors:

1. Actual rental yields.
2. Predicted property prices.

1. Actual Rental Yields

The first factor, actual rental yields, was easy to do. Actual rental yield is:

$$\frac{ACTUAL\ YEARLY\ RENT}{ACTUAL\ PROPERTY\ PRICE} \times 100$$

Since these figures are actuals, I collated all the rental figures from local letting agents in the UK and all the local property prices in the UK from the Land Registry and calculated all the yields being offered from all UK locations. I then eliminated all the poor yielding locations and where I thought tenant demand was low (even if they were high yielding).

2. Predicted Property Prices

Here I did not predict property prices as this is impossible to do. If I could do this I would not be writing this book but buying everything I could in a hotspot area! All I did was to look at what would make an area's property price rise above the national average. I came up with the following:

- Proposed transportation link improvements such as improved road and rail links, expansion of local airports and improved public transport.
- Proposed inward investment from private companies, government and trusts.
- Proposed improvements to leisure facilities such as sport centres, parks and shopping centres.
- The likelihood of holiday seasons being lengthened for holiday areas.
- Our own experience gathered from being in this industry and from comments from letting and estate agents.

What Type of Investor Are You?

So you know you want to invest in property but why and how are you going to do it, there are many ways to invest in property, but we have narrowed these ways down to seven types. Investors can be broadly categorised into the following and it is up to you to decide which category or categories you fit into:

Type	Objective	Description
Cash&Equity Investor	To maximise rental income and capital growth combined. Will also sell home when this further achieves this objective.	This approach is a semi-business approach. The investor has no love for the property but is only interested in the overall money the property is going to make. He will sell if the market is high or hold if the rental income is good. His intentions are to re-invest any monies gained back into another property or properties. This type of investor will have a greater degree of interest in property than other investors as he will stay abreast of the market.
Pension Investor	To cover all costs involved with the house by the rental income and have the house paid off by retirement age. The rental income (or return on sale) thus providing an income thereon.	This investor will be at least 15 years off retirement age. He will look for a property that will always have good rental demand as he intends to live off this rental income when he retires. He may also consider selling the property and using the monies raised to purchase an annuity. If so, he will also look for a high capital growth area. As good practice this type of investor should always evaluate whether their equity in the property can purchase an income greater than the rental income being generated currently.
Retirement Investor	To cover all costs involved with the house by the rental income and have the house paid off by retirement age. Then sell own home to move into the investment home.	Again non-typical investment properties will be sought and he will probably seek properties in a surrounding village of a main town or city. A key concern for this investor is tenant demand so he may well be steered towards villages surrounding main towns and cities. The investor will use the proceeds from the sale of his original home to clear outstanding mortgages and purchase an annuity.
University Investor	To provide a home for son/daughter while at university for 3 years. Sell/hold after 3 years.	The aim of this investor is to purchase a 4+ bedroomed home near the university and get the son or daughter to live in one room and rent the other rooms to his or her friends. The rental income will cover all costs involved with the house and then the house can be sold on for profit or held and rented out again through the university. The overall profit on the investment is the boarding fees saved in the 3 years and the gain on the sale of the property.

Type	Objective	Description
Business Investor	To maximise rental income to replace salary from full-time employment.	The investor will look for high yielding properties so as to replace the lost income from leaving their job. He will invest in only high tenant demand areas as he relies on this income to pay his day-to-day bills. He will be interested in the property market hence he will be abreast of the latest prices, mortgage rates and rental figures. This way he can ensure that his net income is maximised.

From reading this list you will be able to decide what type of investor you are and more importantly what you want to get from your investment. Once you are clear what you want then the whole process becomes easier as you know exactly what you are looking for.

So Which Hotspot Should You Choose?

It is not for me to tell you where to specifically invest. I have short-listed areas where to invest but the rest is up to you. I think you should consider some or all of the following depending on what type of investor you are:

1. In or out of your home town?
2. Proximity to a university.
3. Proximity to a motorway junction.
4. Fashionable addresses.
5. Public transport links.
6. Ex-council properties.
7. School and catchment areas.
8. Shopping facilities and local leisure facilities.
9. Parking.
10. Hospitals.

In Your Home Town

The advantages of buying property locally are many. You know the area well, and may be able to hear of property coming up for sale before it goes to the estate agents. Because of local knowledge you have a 'gut feel' or sixth sense about whether a house in such and such an area will attract which sort of tenants.

Perhaps you can tell which side of the estate or which side of the road is easiest for getting into work or shopping areas using public transport. You don't have to take the word of the estate agent on everything, and I think this gives you more strength sometimes in making your offering to buy. The chances are strong that you can put together a small team of builders, decorators, and repairers to look after the property or portfolio of properties you end up having.

The final benefit of having property close to you is that you can be on hand quicker, and for many landlords this is particularly important. If you are collecting money yourself there are clear benefits. If you are using the services of a letting agent then the location does not matter and you can choose more broadly.

Away From Your Home Town

If you have a house in an area which commands good rent and live yourself in an area where either mortgages or rent are low by comparison, then it is possible for you to benefit strongly by receiving a rental income – even on just one property – that is greater than your own accommodation cost.

A studio flat in a fashionable part of London grosses more rent than a 4 bed house in the outskirts of London. Might this be something for you to explore? Can your lifestyle benefit from a rental income which covers your own biggest bill each month? With the use of telephones and e-mail, particularly if you are self-employed, work in creative or people focused businesses there is far more opportunity than ever before for you to work from home, say three days a week and go to see work colleagues and clients on the other two.

Look at this location topic from a different angle. As a rule of thumb, the further away you are from London the lower the price of most properties. The further you are from an area of a town which is fashionable or desirable, the less you are likely to pay for a property. However, the closer you are to good train networks between cities, or to decent bus and train networks in and around cities, the more attractive your property becomes, no matter how unfashionable the area.

The real value to you in understanding this process is that you can use your money to buy property in towns where property could cost around half of what it might cost to buy in your own area.

Proximity to a University

If the campus is within a mile or two from your flat then you will probably score well here. There will be a strong demand for property that is well maintained, clean, dry and has a good landlord – you! Keep in with the student accommodation office and you could have a steady stream of revenue.

On the other hand, what happens during the ten weeks of summer holiday? Do you spend two weeks decorating it every summer and eight weeks wishing you had full-time tenants, or do you offer the students a slight reduction in rental over the summer period so as to ensure your house is always occupied by someone? Think it through but the location overall could mean you are onto a winner.

Proximity to a Motorway Junction

Provided it is within ten or fifteen minutes' drive this can have a great beneficial impact on your house or flat. Many busy, working people want to be able to get on the road quickly each day for their jobs and this accessibility means you can be assured of a quick turnaround time between tenancies. Generally a plus point and a good move.

Two minutes' drive from the same junction and you should be worrying. If a tenant is renting in a place where they feel the local environment is either too noisy, too smelly or too dangerous they will not stay in your property for long. By inspecting a property at different times of the day you can become aware of the impact of the rush hour on local traffic conditions, where people are using the street as a 'rat run'. But if your tenant market is busy professional people then buy property where they can have quick access to the road networks without living on top of them!

Fashionable Address

Watch out for this one. The more you have to pay for a property the more nervous you get watching the gap between tenancies and the smaller the return on your investment generally. You can get tenants to fill these properties but they have to find the money and corporate lets are only feasible in certain postcode areas. For the majority of the country this is not relevant.

If you want to experience the benefit of capital appreciation but are a little short of the readies to begin with, buy in an adjacent area where the tenants are still close to these fashionable and trendy postcodes but without you having to pay stupid prices for your bricks and mortar. If you can get a rent of £1,000 on an ex-council flat close to a city centre and still retain a healthy profit, why would you want to pay through the nose for only a marginally better rent and use up much of your own investment funds on a heavy deposit? Remember your strategy and stick to it!

Public Transport Links

This is a big one! If your tenants can be on a bus or a train within ten minutes' walk of the property they will be keen to take the property on. Five minutes is of course even better. In the London market anything within five to ten minutes' walk from a tube station will command a better premium for the advantage of that proximity. The same is true of any of the bigger cities with their tram link services across the central routes.

If there are few transport links then ask yourself seriously who you are trying to attract as a tenant. If they do not use transport will they have their own car? Are they working and able to commute to earn their money in order to pay your rent. Will they be so far removed in your property from friends and workmates that after three months they become lonely and move out? Be careful on this one.

Ex-council Properties

Where for many private buyers this does not appeal as a place to make their homes, these are often a landlord's dream. Normally built to a good standard you can buy a lot of bedroom for your pound! Semi-detached and terraced properties are plentiful and rent well to people who want to live and work in an area where they perhaps grew up, or where they can stay close to friends and family. In urban areas ex-council high rise blocks provide the best views around. Your working tenants will get as much space on the city skyline as in many expensive warehouse and industrial building conversions that have cost three or four times as much. Unemployed tenants on the same estate may provide you with an income that – although slow to get started with the Benefit Office – can be as reliable or more reliable than the income from a working tenant.

On the downside you may have one of just a few privately purchased properties within a very large and run down estate. Avoid these. Instead, look to buy flats or maisonettes on the outer edges of such big estates, close to public transport, schools and shopping facilities.

School and Catchment Areas

Where a school has been judged to be of a high standard, parents will move as close as possible to be able to get their child into the school without having to pay for private education. This demand can be very strong and push house prices up significantly close to the school. This means that if you can rent out a property close to such a school you can expect demand to be high from professional people, perhaps on a corporate let. The implication is that you can stand to receive good capital appreciation on your original investment while the tenants cover the mortgage until you want to sell.

Pricing around good schools can be prohibitive to the flow of investing landlords, given they know what margins they want, and can see what the rental sector will stand.

Shopping Facilities and Local Leisure Facilities

Big brand fast food restaurants, out of town shopping centres and good designer pubs within a few miles of your property will again make the rental easier. Where the amenities are of good quality there will be good demand from tenants who want to be able to shop, dine and socialise within a short distance of their new home in your flat or house.

Where there is a lack of such facilities or where shopping is unsafe and streets are awkward after dusk, you will find the rentals equally unattractive. Take care to think why a property is so cheap in the agent's window? Why is it such an apparent bargain at auction?

Parking

With cars so cheap and finance so easy to come by, most of your tenants will be drivers with at least one car. If you are letting to a couple or to a group of friends who share the tenancy, there may be two or three cars that need to park nearby. This is fine if you have a large driveway to the property or if there is plenty of land around the house. But being realistic this may not be the case. Get properties where parking outside is straightforward – either on a driveway or at the roadside.

Where parking is difficult, where roads are narrow and driving is cramped, things can work against the rental of the property. People are territorial animals and like to park their cars within a hundred yards of their house, if not right outside. Narrow streets and few parking bays simply cause more aggravation. No one wants to go to their car in the morning and find a wing mirror smashed or a body panel scratched.

Hospitals

Just like having a university near to your investment, a hospital on your doorstep can be a great source of tenants and the effective route to some consistent rental cash flow. Hospitals have their own accommodation teams to help staff find a place to sleep, so make friends with such people and keep your properties in good condition.

The fastest way to be thrown off the list of a hospital accommodation office is to misrepresent your property or to not maintain it once you have hospital staff renting from you. No-one likes a bad landlord and the message spreads fast.

Property Viewing Record

I have created a Property Viewing Record that can be a useful aide-memoire to have with you when going to look at potential investments:

Property Viewing Record				
Estate Agent/Auctioneer				
Address of the property				
Type of Property				
Asking Price				
Date of first viewing				
Date of second visit				
Comments about the Surrounding Area				
Schools	Traffic Noise	Shops	Public Transport	Business Units
Outside				
Garden and Driveway				
Garage				
Window Frames/Glass				
Walls				
Drains/Guttering				
Roof				
Neighbouring Properties				

Inside
Hallway
Lounge
Dining Room
Kitchen
Utility Room
Bedroom 1 (Sizes)
Bedroom 2
Bedroom 3
Bedroom 4
Bathroom
Loft
Potential Work Required
Heating and Plumbing
Electrical Repair
Decoration
Damp Patches
External Lighting
General Observations/Things to Remember

And Finally...

These are a few little pointers that I have learned that should help you along the way:

- Avoid the common mistake of purchasing a property because you like the look of it or think it is cute! Instead put your money into one which will appeal strongly to tenants.

- Buy the local newspapers and gazettes on the day they advertise local property. If you don't live in the area ask them to send you this on a weekly basis.

- Telephone all the agents and ask them to recommend the areas which rent the best and the most consistently.

- Get on the agent's mailing list as a potential investor, and ask for their landlords pack. This will include details of property they have for rent, and property suitable for a rental investment. This way you can do your homework from one mailing.

- Tell the agent you work to strict pricing/bedroom criteria and hold your ground. Most agents will always send you the properties at the top end of your budget because they make more commission this way. Find an agent you can trust to bring you good deals. Watch out for them trying to promote all the one bed studio flats and maisonettes they can find. This is fine if you are looking at a city with a very fluid population and you are buying in the central district because you want to rent to urban dwelling city workers seeking tiny *pied-à-terre* properties. Elsewhere however think carefully about this type of unit and the difficulties that come with it.

- Using your criteria for return on investment select a half dozen properties and tour round them with your agent. Don't be afraid to take photographs or video, or to use a small dictating machine to record your impressions of each property.

- Make notes about the street it is in as well as about neighbouring properties.

- Never visit any property outside of full daylight. This is safer for you but it also means you see things as they are. You have every right to take a friend or adviser with you on these property tours. They will see things you never notice. This could save you a lot of time and money wasted. Always have either a camera or a video camera with you when you go to see properties. By the time you are ten minutes away from the house you have just seen, you will have forgotten half the features, or be unable to recall the colour of the woodwork.

Good Luck!

Ajay Ahuja

How to Use the Property Hotspot Profiles

Before you explore all the property hotspot profiles I've prepared for you, here is an explanation of what headings I used for each hotspot, what they mean and why I've included them.

Heading	Description	Why included
Area:	The area in the UK where the hotspot is.	You need to know where the hotspot is!
Category:	The quality of the hotspot – see above under heading 'What is a Hotspot' for definitions.	Some hotspots are better than others. I have graded them to help you fit them in with your own personal goals.
Postcode:	The postcode sector the area falls into.	Postcodes can have a powerful impact on property prices. See power of postcodes chapter below.
In congestion zone:	Whether the area falls into the congestion zone charging zone and if not how far away from the zone it is.	The impact of whether an area is in the zone or not can be quite significant. See chapter on congestion zone below.
Parking & Traffic:	The availability of parking in the area.	Parking availability can affect property prices.
Ethnicity Bias:	Whether there is a significant ethnic community in the area.	To help the reader gauge the whole feel of the area.
Investor profile:	The investor profiles which the area is suited to. The seven types of investor are above – see 'The Seven Types of Investor' for definitions.	There's no point looking at a hotspot if it doesn't fit the type of investor you are. Ensure that the hotspot is relevant to you.
Crime:	*Violence* – Acts of violence against a person *Sexual* – Sexual assaults on a person *Burglary* – Burglaries from dwellings *Motor* – Theft of motor vehicles	Gives you an idea of the scale of crime in the area across the key types of crime that can affect property prices.

▶

Heading	Description	Why included
Per 1000 population:	The number of reported crimes defined above per thousand population.	
Yield range:	The range of yields that can be expected from this area. Yield being: (Annual Rental Income) divided by (Purchase Price of Property) x 100.	At a glance to see if the area can offer you the yields you require based on your investment plan.
Price ranges – *Low*	The lowest purchase price expected for the type of property in question.	A guide price for the cheapest property available in the area.
Price ranges – *Hi*	The highest purchase price expected for the type of property in question.	A guide price for the most expensive property available in the area.
Price ranges – *Low £pw*	The lowest rental figure per week expected for the type of property in question.	A guide price for the cheapest rental figure available in the area.
Price ranges – *Hi £pw*	The highest rental figure per week expected for the type of property in question.	A guide price for the most expensive rental figure available in the area.
Price ranges – *Low*	The lowest yield expected for the type of property in question.	What you can expect in the worst case scenario.
Price ranges – *Hi*	The highest yield expected for the type of property in question.	What you can expect in the best case scenario.
Studios	Studio flats have one room and a kitchen and a bathroom. These are typically leasehold properties without gardens.	I have segregated the types of property for you to closer identify and analyse the property prices. Some yields are better for the different types of properties. This can then direct you to these type of properties thus maximising your possible yield.
1 bed flat	1 bed flats have a living room, a bedroom, a kitchen and a bathroom. These are typically leasehold properties without gardens.	
2 bed flat	2 bed flats have a living room, two bedrooms, a kitchen and a bathroom. These are typically leasehold properties without gardens.	
2 bed house	2 bed houses have a living room, two bedrooms, a kitchen and a bathroom. These are typically freehold properties with gardens.	
3 bed house	3 bed houses have a living room, three bedrooms and a bathroom. These are typically freehold properties with gardens.	

Heading	Description	Why included
Valuations above the national average by:	The valuation of the homes in the area relative to the rest of the UK. The calculation being: (Average Price of Property in Area − Average Price of Property in UK) divided by (Average Price of Property in UK) x 100	It's a good benchmark to see how good the area is. If the valuation is above the national average then the area will tend to be a better area.
Capital growth last 12 months:	(Average Price for Quarter 4 2002 − Average Property Price for Quarter 4 2002) divided by (Average Property Price for Quarter 4 2001) x 100	It's good to see the growth that has occurred in the last 12 months − has it seen a boom? Has it not grown and is ready to boom? Is it on the way down? But remember that past performance is no indication of future performance.
Capital growth last 4 years: Note: when data permits the 5 year growth is stated	(Average Price for Quarter 4 2002 − Average Property Price for Quarter 4 1998) divided by (Average Property Price for Quarter 4 1998) x 100	It's good to see the growth that has occurred in the last 4 years property is a long term investment. However you can still ask − has it seen a boom? Has it not grown and is ready to boom? Is it on the way down? But remember that past performance is no indication of future performance.
Tube:	The nearest underground tube station in the area.	If an area has a tube station it can have a massive effect on its popularity. See proposed tube stations chapter below.
Demand For letting:	In our own professional opinion what we think the likely demand is for rental properties.	If you want a non-quantative opinion then here it is!
Average void period:	In our own professional opinion what we think the likely time the property will be un let between tenancies.	If you want a quantative opinion then here it is!
Capital Growth (out of 5)	Our own total score out of five for the area based on *predicted* capital growth.	It's why I invest − I want my money to grow. A simple score out of 5 should help you.
Yield (out of 5)	Our own total score out of five for the area based on *actual* yield.	Another reason why I invest − I want money now! A simple score out of 5 should help you.
Out of 10	Our own total score out of ten for the area based on capital growth and yield. See below.	Everyone loves a score out of 10. It gives you an idea of the quality of the hotspot in numerical format.
Summary:	A brief summary of the area without needing to read the whole description below.	For the lazy. The area summed up in a nut shell.

Heading	Description	Why included
Sought After Streets:	The best streets to buy in.	You need to know where to specifically look.
Description:	A full description of the area and why it is a hotspot.	For the serious. The detail for the area to help you make a more informed choice.
Estate agents:	The estate agents that serve the area.	So you like the area – this is where you find the properties!
Letting agents:	The letting agents that serve the area.	So you've got the property – you need to let it! These organisations will help you.

A–Z of Property Hotspots in London

Area:	Acton			
Catergory:	A			
Postcode:	W3			
In Congestion Zone:	No – 7.2 miles outside.			
Parking and Traffic:	Free, Permits & Meters. Uxbridge Road can get congested.			
Ethnicity Bias:	Asian			
Investor Profile:	Pension, Business, Cash&Equity,			
Crime:	Violence	Sexual	Burglary	Motor
Per 1000 population:	22	1	10	8
Yield Range:	6.2% – 9.4%			

Price Ranges	Low £	Hi £	Low £pw	Hi £pw	Low	Hi
Studio flat	80,000	100,000	130	180	8.5%	9.4%
1 bed flat	125,000	170,000	170	220	6.7%	7.1%
2 bed flat	160,000	220,000	200	310	6.5%	7.3%
2 bed house	180,000	250,000	225	325	6.5%	6.8%
3 bed house	220,000	375,000	300	450	6.2%	7.1%

Valuations above the London average by:	–5.6% (£228,216)	
	Actual	London Average
Capital growth last 12 months:	13.5%	19%
Capital growth last 48 months:	58.0%	89%
Tube:	**Acton Town**. District & Piccidilly Lines (Zone 3) – 20 mins to Piccidilly Circus and 23 mins to Victoria	
Demand For Letting:	Good	
Average void period:	7 days	

	Capital Growth (out of 5)	Yield (out of 5)	Total (out of 10)
Our rating:	3	3	6

Summary:	A safe bet with great communications.
Sought After Streets:	Rosemont Rd, Mill Hill Rd & Pierrepoint Rd.
Description:	This area is the cheap alternative to the very exclusive Bedford Park and Ealing but this is where the value lies – you get a lot for your money. It is not an area just made up of council blocks. There are several pockets of Victorian homes and converted apartments dotted around that make very good professional rentals. The Tudor estate has a number of reasonably priced flats which are a hit with the younger professionals.

	The is a high percentage (around 35%) of ethnic minorities – mainly Asian (because of its proximity to Southall and Ealing) and Japanese (because of the Japanese school in the area). There are also a lot of Antipidians (Australians, New Zealanders & South Africans) in the area because of the availability of affordable multi-lets in large converted buildings.			
	The high street, Acton High St, has secured a grant for a complete revamp and regeneration of the street which will make the whole feel of the area more welcoming. If you can afford it then take a trip to Poets Corner – it is the visual definition of the word 'gentrification'.			
	Your money is safe in this area. It has great links to the A40 and M4 which take you to Heathrow and Oxford, there are plenty of large Blue Chip employers in and surrounding Acton and there is a certain buzz to the area which will ensure that rental demand will always be strong and that rental values will hold.			
Estate Agents:	**Name**	**Address**	**Tel**	**Web**
	Ravenscourt Residential	3 Seven Stars Corner, Paddenswick Road, Acton, London, W12 8ET	020 8740 5678	www.ravens court residential.co.uk
	Churchill Agencies Ltd	18 Old Oak Common Lane, Acton, London, W3 7EL	020 8749 9798	www.churchill estates.co.uk
	Hart International Ltd	76 Old Oak Common Lane, Acton, London, W3 7DA	020 8743 4488	www.hart estateagents. co.uk
	Barnard Marcus	9 The Broadway, Gunnersbury Lane, Acton, London, W3 8HZ	020 8992 6868	www.sequence home.co.uk
	Japan Services	2 Queens Drive, West Acton, London, W3 0HA	020 8752 0445	www.japan services.co.uk
	Robertson, Smith & Kempton	98 High Street, Acton, London, W3 6QX	020 8896 3996	www.rsk homes.co.uk
	Citydeals Estates (London) Ltd	113 Churchfield Road, Acton, London, W3 6AH	020 8896 1993	www.city dealestates.com

▶

Letting Agents:	Name	Address	Tel	Web
	London Tokyo Property Services Ltd	2 Station Parade, Noel Road, London, W3 0DS	020 8992 6818	www.london-tokyo.co.uk
	Standard Lettings	4 Station Parade, Gunnersbury Lane, London, W3 8HN	020 8752 1800	www.standard lettings.co.uk
	Citydeals Estates (London) Ltd	113 Churchfield Road, London, W3 6AH	020 8896 1993	www.citydeal estates.com
	Access Residential	11 The Vale, Acton, London, W3 7SH	020 8743 7234	No website
	Vistastar (Acton) Ltd	53 High St, Acton, London, W3 6ND	020 8993 8807	www.finder property.com
	Central Residential Ltd	11 The Vale, London, W3 7SH	020 8743 7234	No website
	Japan Letting Agency	177 High St, Acton, London, W3 9DJ	020 8993 6100	No website

Area:	**Barnes**			
Catergory:	C			
Postcode:	SW13			
In Congestion Zone:	No – 6.0 miles outside.			
Parking and Traffic:	Permits & Meters. No significant traffic trouble spots.			
Ethnicity Bias:	Swedish			
Investor Profile:	Pension, Business, Cash&Equity, Retirement.			
Crime:	Violence	Sexual	Burglary	Motor
Per 1000 population:	11	1	6	3
Yield Range:	5.2% – 10.2%			

Price Ranges	Low £	Hi £	Low £pw	Hi £pw	Low	Hi
Studio flat	95,000	135,000	155	205	7.9%	8.5%
1 bed flat	140,000	245,000	195	275	5.8%	7.2%
2 bed flat	178,000	325,000	240	640	7.0%	10.2%
2 bed house	250,000	325,000	310	385	6.2%	6.4%
3 bed house	327,000	600,000	325	650	5.2%	5.6%

Valuations above the London average by:	97.1% (£476,632)	
	Actual	**London Average**
Capital growth last 12 months:	12.5%	19%
Capital growth last 48 months:	146.7%	89%
Tube:	None. **Barnes Rail Station** (Zone 3) – 19 minutes to Waterloo.	
Demand For Letting:	Good	
Average void period:	10 days	

	Capital Growth (out of 5)	Yield (out of 5)	Total (out of 10)
Our rating:	3	4	**7**

Summary:	A very pretty place and with good yields – if you can afford it!
Sought After Streets:	Castelnau, Rocks Lane & Church Rd.
Description:	I was first introduced to Barnes by my friend who used to live there and I was amazed at its beauty, exclusivity and insularity. This place does not seem like London by any stretch of the imagination. It's nestled between water (River Thames) and grass (Barnes Common) with elegant Victorian and Edwardian terraced houses lining the wide streets of the area.

The properties are expensive considering there is no tube, but this may be why, because it is a great escape. Once over Hammersmith Bridge you are in peaceful Barnes in full knowledge that you can just as easily go back to the hustle and bustle of city life in a short bus ride back over the bridge. This makes properties highly sought after from people having to work in the city but still require a certain level of country living (like me!).

The yields are surprisingly good. You are getting great properties with near double digit yields for certain types of properties at the top end. There is high demand from the Swedes due to the Swedish School being located in Barnes. It is also a desired area by people in the media and internet industry (which includes my friend) and affluent families. Word on the street is that there is a shortage of 4-5 bedroomed houses available for rent so premium prices can be charged.

There are plans for an £18m sports centre to be constructed which should boost the influx of people in to the area. I consider this to be a good thing as it will increase the amenities in the area making it a more popular place to live.

The high street is chain free! Independent deli's, boutiques and a la carte restaurants occupy the key commercial roads which all add to the exclusive feel to the area.

Estate Agents:	Name	Address	Tel	Web
	Allen Briegel	67 Barnes High Street, Barnes, London, SW13 9LD	020 8392 1635	www.allen briegel.co.uk
	Susan Porter Property Management	25 Castelnau, Barnes, London, SW13 9RP	020 8748 2040	No Website
	A H Properties	88 Lowther Road, Barnes, London, SW13 9NW	020 8741 2224	No website
	Boileau Braxton	135 Church Road, Barnes, London, SW13 9HR	020 8741 7400	www.property finder.co.uk
	Laurent Residential	6 Charlotte Road, Barnes, London, SW13 9QJ	020 8563 7925	www.laurent residential.co.uk
	James Anderson	64 Barnes High Street, Barnes, London, SW13 9LD	020 8876 0100	www.james anderson.co.uk

Letting Agents:	Name	Address	Tel	Web
	C Howard King & Partners	2 Barnes High Street, London, SW13 9LB	020 8878 7966	www.howard-king.co.uk
	Sargent & Young		020 8878 1115	www.finda property.co./ sargent
	Laurent Residential	6 Charlotte Road, Barnes, London, SW13 9QJ	020 8563 7925	www.laurent residential.co.uk
	Dixon Porter Ltd	202 Upper Richmond Road West, East Sheen, London, SW14 8AN	020 8878 2828	www.dixon porter.co.uk
	James Anderson	4 Parkway House, Sheen Lane, East Sheen, London, SW14 8LS	020 8876 6611	www.james anderson.co.uk

Area:	**Bethnal Green**			
Catergory:	A			
Postcode:	E2			
In Congestion Zone:	No – 1.5 miles outside.			
Parking and Traffic:	Permits & Meters. No significant traffic trouble spots.			
Ethnicity Bias:	Asian			
Investor Profile:	Pension, Business, Cash&Equity, University			
Crime:	Violence	Sexual	Burglary	Motor
Per 1000 population:	35	2	10	27
Yield Range:	6.2% – 9.9%			

Price Ranges	Low £	Hi £	Low £pw	Hi £pw	Low	Hi
Studio flat	87,000	97,000	135	185	8.1%	9.9%
1 bed flat	95,000	175,000	175	260	7.7%	9.5%
2 bed flat	145,000	280,000	210	360	6.7%	7.5%
2 bed house	210,000	310,000	260	420	6.4%	7.0%
3 bed house	260,000	400,000	310	490	6.2%	6.4%

Valuations above the London average by:	−5.6% (£228,249)	
	Actual	London Average
Capital growth last 12 months:	16.2%	19%
Capital growth last 48 months:	99.9%	89%
Tube:	**Bethnal Green**. Central Line (Zone 2) – 17 mins to Oxford Street	
Demand For Letting:	Excellent	
Average void period:	1 week	

	Capital Growth (out of 5)	Yield (out of 5)	Total (out of 10)
Our rating:	4	4	**8**

Summary:	Extremely close to the City with excellent rental yields – could be the next 'Farringdon'.
Sought After Streets:	Corfield St, Millenium Place – Cambridge Heath Rd, Hackney Rd, Moravian St & Globe Rd.
Description:	I find this place amazing. It is a £3 cab ride or a 3 minute tube journey and you are in Liverpool Street, the heart of the financial capital of the world! Yet the area looks run down in places with only a few pockets of 'nice' areas. The nice areas being the old ex-local authority Victorian flats such as Corfield Street off Bethnal Green High Road which are no

▶

more than 5 storeys high, loft conversion flats springing up by developers from disused schools and warehouses and newly builds such as Millennium Place opposite Cambridge Heath Station.

These areas are highly sought after by the young professionals who work in the city. This has led to both property and rental prices rising in proportion with each other, hence the decent yields of nearly 10% in some areas. I think these young professionals do not mind taking the risk in living in these east-end ex-gangster type of areas as they get a lot more for their money. Shoreditch is only a brief stroll down Bethnal Green High Road and there they enter into the trendy-bar city where other young professional 20-somethings meet up.

Tenant demand will be strong if our financial economy is strong as this area relies on jobs being provided by the city. Currently the state of the financial economy seems good for at least the next 12 months but be aware this can change quite rapidly. In the last 6 years the number of jobs in London have grown by 17% but we are heavily linked to the US economy so it pays to keep abreast of what's going on across the Atlantic.

Queen Marys Hospital & College is a 5 minute walk and hence the area proves to popular with the medical students. The college is keen to hear from landlords as there is a shortage of student accommodation and offer a fee free tenant finding service.

I think out of all the areas in London I think this area will be radically different in 20 years to what it is today. It is ripe for gentrification and is within distance of the burgeoning financial city to be gobbled up and turned in a support centre of hotels, restaurants and bars for international business visitors.

Estate Agents:	Name	Address	Tel	Web
	Land & Co	485–487 Bethnal Green Road, Bethnal Green, London, E2 9QH	020 7729 1815	www.land andco.co.uk
	W J Meade	492 Bethnal Green Road, London, E2 0EA	020 7729 4360	www.wj meade.co.uk
	Express Homes	2 Approach Road, Bethnal Green, London, E2 9LY	020 8981 8526	No Website
	Global Estate Agents	475 Bethnal Green Road, London, E2 9QH	020 7729 6767	www.finda property.co.uk

Estate Agents:	Name	Address	Tel	Web
	Cityfish Property Services	121 Bethnal Green Road, London, E2 7DG	020 7739 1414	www.cityfish property.com
	Hamilton Fox Estate Agents	488 Bethnal Green Road, London, E2 0EA	020 7729 8777	www.hamilton fox.co.uk

Letting Agents:	Name	Address	Tel	Web
	Alan Harvey Property Services	462 Roman Road, Bow, London, E3 5LU	020 8980 1111	www.alan harvey.co.uk
	W J Meade	490–492 Bethnal Green Road, London, E2 0EA	020 7729 4360	www.wj meade.co.uk
	Londons People Property Services	41 Roman Road, Bethnal Green, London, E2 0HU	020 8981 9292	No website
	Major Properties Ltd	71 Temple Street, London, E2 6QQ	020 7739 1600	No website
	Stephen James	8a Hackney Road, London, E2 7NS	020 7739 4300	www.stephen james.net
	Abiba Lettings	283a Kingsland Road, London, E2 8AS	0845 130 0225	www.abiba. azizalettings. co.uk

Area:	Belsize Park			
Catergory:	C			
Postcode:	NW3			
In Congestion Zone:	No – 3.3 miles outside.			
Parking and Traffic:	Permits & Meters. No significant traffic trouble spots.			
Ethnicity Bias:	None			
Investor Profile:	Pension, Business, Cash&Equity, University			
Crime:	**Violence**	**Sexual**	**Burglary**	**Motor**
Per 1000 population:	27	2	16	11
Yield Range:	4.9% – 6.5%			

Price Ranges	Low £	Hi £	Low £pw	Hi £pw	Low	Hi
Studio flat	120,000	250,000	150	300	6.2%	6.5%
1 bed flat	195,000	350,000	230	440	6.1%	6.5%
2 bed flat	265,000	650,000	320	700	5.6%	6.3%
2 bed house	370,000	700,000	400	850	5.6%	6.3%
3 bed house	500,000	1,300,000	475	1450	4.9%	5.8%

Valuations above the London average by:	97.1% (£476,700)	
	Actual	**London Average**
Capital growth last 12 months:	4.8%	19%
Capital growth last 48 months:	125.1%	89%
Tube:	**Belsize Park** Northern Line (Zone 2) – 14 mins to Euston.	
Demand For Letting:	**Excellent**	
Average void period:	2 days	

	Capital Growth (out of 5)	Yield (out of 5)	Total (out of 10)
Our rating:	4	2	**6**

Summary:	A little area with big promise.
Sought After Streets:	Belsize Lane, Haverstock Hill & Belsize Avenue.
Description:	The next best thing to Hampstead! This is being slowly realised and the prices being achieved for some properties are unbelievable. There seems to be things happening in reverse – converted flats are being turned back into houses.
	The area is not cheap, so yields are not the best. I chose this area for capital growth as it will cash in on the Hampstead name. The properties

▶

here are of equivalent quality to Hampstead, but do not carry the exorbitant prices.

The great thing about this place that even though it is a relatively small area (the smallest in this book), it still has its own tube station. So what more do you want? – everyone wants to live here, it has the name, it has a tube and it is just about affordable!

The area is becoming more and more international with the inflow coming from business executives with their families on short to medium term contracts seeking a nice place to live in.

Estate Agents:	Name	Address	Tel	Web
	Hadleigh Residential	19 Belsize Grove, London, NW3 4TX	020 7722 9799	www.hadleigh .co.uk
	Heywoods Estate Agents	27 Belsize Lane, London, NW3 5AS	020 7794 0005	www.heywoods .net
	Lexingtons	35 Belsize Lane, London, NW3 5AS	020 7435 7775	www.lexingtons .com
	Winkworth & Co	92 Heath Street, London, NW3 1DP	020 7794 1155	www.winkworth .co.uk
	Kinleigh Folkard & Hayward	38 Englands Lane, Belsize Park, London NW3 4UE	020 7483 4302	www.kfh.co.uk
	Amberden Estates	6, South Hill Park London NW3 2SB	020 7433 3310	www.amberdon .co.uk

Letting Agents:	Name	Address	Tel	Web
	Kinleigh Folkard & Hayward	38 Englands Lane, Belsize Park, London, NW3 4UE	020 7586 9006	www.kfh.co.uk
	Hamptons International	21 Heath Street, London, NW3 6TR	020 7431 4462	www.hamptons .co.uk
	Benham & Reeves Residential Lettings	51–53 Heath Street, Hampstead, London, NW3 6UG	020 7435 9681	www.ben hamreeves lettings.co.uk

▶

Letting Agents:	Name	Address	Tel	Web
	Anscombe & Ringland	55 Heath Street, Hampstead, London, NW3 6UG	020 7794 1151	www.chancellors.co.uk
	Jeffersons Management Services	124 Finchley Road, Hampstead, London, NW3 5HT	020 7794 0091	www.jeffersons.uk.net
	Behr & Butchoff	5 Holly Hill, Hampstead, London, NW3 6QN	020 7431 7222	www.behrandbutchoff.com
	Chesterton Residential	9 Heath Street, Hampstead, London, NW3 6TP	020 7794 1125	www.chesterton.co.uk
	Heathgate	105 Heath Street, Hampstead, London, NW3 6SS	020 7435 3344	www.heathgate.com

Area:	**Bermondsey**			
Catergory:	B			
Postcode:	SE16			
In Congestion Zone:	No – 0.3 miles outside.			
Parking and Traffic:	Permits & Meters. Odd places free. No significant traffic trouble spots.			
Ethnicity Bias:	None			
Investor Profile:	Pension, Business, Cash&Equity, University			
Crime:	Violence	Sexual	Burglary	Motor
Per 1000 population:	33	2	14	12
Yield Range:	6.8% – 11.4%			

Price Ranges	Low £	Hi £	Low £pw	Hi £pw	Low	Hi
Studio flat	115,000	185,000	150	295	6.8%	8.3%
1 bed flat	125,000	260,000	210	490	8.7%	9.8%
2 bed flat	150,000	290,000	260	1,100	9.0%	9.0%
2 bed house	175,000	300,000	325	525	9.1%	9.7%
3 bed house	200,000	380,000	440	700	9.6%	11.4%

Valuations above the London average by:	–6.4% (£226,282)	
	Actual	London Average
Capital growth last 12 months:	27.0%	19%
Capital growth last 48 months:	91.0%	89%
Tube:	**Bermondsey** Jubilee Line (Zone 2) – 3 mins to London Bridge and 9 mins to Westminster	
Demand For Letting:	Good	
Average void period:	6 days	

	Capital Growth (out of 5)	Yield (out of 5)	Total (out of 10)
Our rating:	4	4	8

Summary:	Offering both strong yields and potential growth which is unique. One of the few areas that has the ability to deliver big returns from both angles.
Sought After Streets:	Mill Street, Jamaica Road and Bermondsey Wall East.
Description:	This used to be a horrible place. About 10 years ago the area looked like a scene out of a gangster movie. There are still places like that but the area has cleaned up a lot. The area serves Canary Wharf and the city and is linked by the relatively new tube station.

There are plenty of developments occurring in this area and there is a respectable cluster of shops and restaurants at nearby Shad Thames. These areas are highly sought after by the young professionals who work in the city. This has led to both property and rental prices rising in proportion with each other hence the decent yields of nearly 10% in some areas. I think these young professionals do not mind taking the risk in living in these ex-gangster type of areas as they get a lot more for their money.

Tenant demand will be strong if our financial economy is strong as this area relies on jobs being provided by Canary Wharf and the city. Currently the state of the financial economy seems good for at least the next 12 months but be aware this can change quite rapidly. In the last 6 years the number of jobs in London have grown by 17% but we are heavily linked to the US economy so it pays to keep abreast of what's going on across the Atlantic.

Estate Agents:	Name	Address	Tel	Web
	Williams Lynch	90 Bermondsey Street, London, SE1 3UB	020 7407 4100	www.williams lynch.co.uk
	Daniel Cobb	82–84 Bermondsey Street, London, SE1 3UD	020 7357 0026	www.daniel cobb.co.uk
	Acorn Estate Agents	118 Bermondsey Street, London, SE1 3TX	020 7089 6565	www.acorn.ltd.uk
	Kalmars Residential	Bermondsey House, 165 Bermondsey Street, London, SE1 3UW	020 7940 7980	www.kalmars .com
Letting Agents:	Name	Address	Tel	Web
	Daniel Cobb	82–84 Bermondsey Street, London, SE1 3UD	020 7357 0026	www.daniel cobb.co.uk
	The County Hall Letting Co	Spice Quay, 34 Shad Thames, London, SE1 2YG	020 7234 0666	www.county hall.co.uk
	Property Liaisons of London Ltd	1 Wapping Wall, Wapping, London, E1 3ST	020 7680 0222	www.property liaisons.co.uk
	Chesterton Residential	220 Tower Bridge Road, London, SE1 2UP	020 7357 6911	www.chesterton .co.uk

Area:	Camden			
Catergory:	C			
Postcode:	NW1			
In Congestion Zone:	No – 1.7 miles outside.			
Parking and Traffic:	Permits & Meters. High Street & Chalk Farm Road gets congested especially at weekends.			
Ethnicity Bias:	None			
Investor Profile:	Pension, Business, Cash&Equity, University			
Crime:	Violence	Sexual	Burglary	Motor
Per 1000 population:	27	2	16	10
Yield Range:	3.8% – 9.7%			

Price Ranges	Low £	Hi £	Low £pw	Hi £pw	Low	Hi
Studio flat	100,000	195,000	155	225	6.0%	8.1%
1 bed flat	150,000	425,000	190	310	3.8%	6.6%
2 bed flat	225,000	550,000	220	530	5.0%	5.1%
2 bed house	275,000	650,000	320	515	4.1%	6.1%
3 bed house	365,000	750,000	425	1400	6.1%	9.7%

Valuations above the London average by:	56.1% (377,391)	
	Actual	**London Average**
Capital growth last 12 months:	171.2%	19%
Capital growth last 48 months:	200.2%	89%
Tube:	**Camden Town** Northern Line (Zone 2) – 6 minutes to Kings Cross, 19 minutes to Oxford Circus.	
Demand For Letting:	**Excellent**	
Average void period:	3 days	

	Capital Growth (out of 5)	Yield (out of 5)	Total (out of 10)
Our rating:	4	2	**6**

Summary:	Excellent tenant demand with astronomical capital growth. Camden is here to stay!
Sought After Streets:	Jamestown Rd, Mornington Terrace, Kentish Town Road & Arlington Rd.
Description:	Everyone wants to live here! And when they do move here they never leave. Prices are expensive as you would expect from a highly desired area. This is home for the media workers, publishers, designers and intellectuals – the trendy, fashionable and rich. There are not many city boys here as Camden is a bit too cosmopolitan for them.

There will be a new shopping complex to be built at and around the station by 2007 and the high street is getting a revamp. Adding this to the already world famous market will only further enhance the appeal of the area. The station will also be able to take you direct to Heathrow and Paris which will add to its cosmopolitan feel.

Rental ranges are wide as the range of properties is wide. Have a long chat with letting agents as the achievable rents for similar looking properties vary widely. There have been lots of new housing developments springing up but they have been a bit pricey. Due to prices falling in London you may be able to get a good discount on their current advertised prices.

Estate Agents:	Name	Address	Tel	Web
	Hotblack Desiato	67 Parkway, Regents Park, Camden, London, NW1 7PP	020 7482 2894	www.hotblackdesiato.co.uk
	Cardoe Martin	40–42 Osnaburgh Street, Camden, London, NW1 3ND	020 7874 1073	www.cardoemartin.co.uk
	David Birkett Estate Agents	119 Regents Park Road, Camden, London, NW1 8UR	020 7722 3094	www.davidbirkett.co.uk
	Camden Bus Estate Agents	27a Parkway, Camden Town, London, NW1 7PN	020 7485 7485	www.camdenbus.co.uk
	Ammo London	63, Chalton St London NW1 1HY	0800 3761195	www.ammolondon.com
	Sandfords	36 Ivor Place, Regents Park, London NW1 6EA	020 7723 9988	www.sandfords.com

Letting Agents:	Name	Address	Tel	Web
	Alexanders	35 Ivor Place, London, NW1 6EA	020 7402 0066	www.alexanders-uk.com
	Michael Charles Lettings	66 Parkway, Camden, London, NW1 7AH	020 7428 0520	www.findaproperty.com

▶

Letting Agents:	Name	Address	Tel	Web
	Stickley & Kent	99–101 Parkway, London, NW1 7PP	020 7267 2053	www.copping joyce.co.uk
	Regents Park Property Services Ltd	107 Regents Park Road, Primrose Hill, London, NW1 8UR	020 7722 8876	www.lettings london.com
	John D Wood & Co Lettings	166 Regent's Park Road, London, NW1 8XN	020 7586 9882	www.johnd wood.co.uk
	David Birkett Estate Agents	119 Regents Park Road, London NW1 8UR	020 7722 3094	www.david birkett.co.uk
	London Tokyo Property Services Ltd	214, Baker St London NW1 5RT	020 7486 4256	www.london-tokyo.co.uk

Area:	Chiswick			
Catergory:	C			
Postcode:	W4			
In Congestion Zone:	No – 6.5 miles outside.			
Parking and Traffic:	Permits & Meters. A4, Hogarth Roundabout and Chiswick High Road gets congested throughout the day.			
Ethnicity Bias:	None			
Investor Profile:	Pension, Business, Cash&Equity, Retirement.			
Crime:	Violence	Sexual	Burglary	Motor
Per 1000 population:	27	1	9	7
Yield Range:	5.8% – 9.0%			

Price Ranges	Low £	Hi £	Low £pw	Hi £pw	Low	Hi
Studio flat	95,000	185,000	165	230	6.5%	9.0%
1 bed flat	140,000	265,000	200	360	7.1%	7.4%
2 bed flat	220,000	460,000	310	550	6.2%	7.3%
2 bed house	235,000	425,000	300	475	5.8%	6.6%
3 bed house	290,000	460,000	370	700	6.6%	7.9%

Valuations above the London average by:	62.9% (£393,971)	
	Actual	**London Average**
Capital growth last 12 months:	7.3%	19%
Capital growth last 48 months:	94.5%	89%

Tube:	**Turnham Green** District Line (Zone 2) – 22 minutes to Embankment.		
Demand For Letting:	Good		
Average void period:	8 days		
	Capital Growth (out of 5)	**Yield** (out of 5)	**Total** (out of 10)
Our rating:	3	3	**6**
Summary:	Pretty area with properties readily available.		
Sought After Streets:	Great Chertsey Rd, Pumping Station Rd & Great West Rd.		
Description:	This is one of the few places in London you can retire to. It has a village feel. You're near the river, there's great architecture, close to Heathrow and the main roads out of London and you're only 6 miles from the centre of town. It has a village feel because it was an old village but this place is now expanding.		

▶

There is a new business park, Chiswick Business Park, which is a hi-tech business park housing established as well as young companies and employing over 7,000 people. I think that the business park will undoubtedly succeed as Chiswick is a great place to live and work. Rental demand will be good from this hi-tech sector as many of the staff will be contractors looking for good rental properties.

The area is predominately family type houses and they are quite expensive, as you can see above. But let's not forget that the rents are not bad and if you find a young family to move in they're unlikely to leave. The growth in prices has slowed down in the last year which has been good for would-be investors. The market is less frantic and there is a ready available stock of homes all offering a sensible yield.

Estate Agents:	Name	Address	Tel	Web
	Fitz-Gibbon Residential	1 Sutton Court Road, Chiswick, London, W4 4NF	020 8995 3335	www.fitz gibbon.co.uk
	Michael Richards & Co	401 Chiswick High Road, Chiswick, London, W4 4AS	020 8994 8512	www.michael richards.uk.com
	Rowan Property Services	19 Ravenscroft Road, Chiswick, London, W4 5EQ	020 8747 9651	No Website
	Bellenger-Locke	33 Bullo Lane, Chiswick, London, W4 5LR	020 8995 5559	www.bellengers .co.uk
	Hartswood Property Management Limited	10 Bedford Corner The Avenue, Chiswick, London, W4 1LD	020 8994 8400	www.hartswood property.co.uk
	Bushells	68–70 Turnham Green Terrace, Chiswick, London, W4 1QN	020 8995 9394	www.bushells .com
	John Spencer Estate Agents	388 Chiswick High Road, Chiswick, London, W4 5TF	020 8995 4321	www.john spencer.co.uk

Letting Agents:	Name	Address	Tel	Web
	Lauristons	229b Chiswick High Road, Chiswick, London, W4 2DW	020 8994 4433	www.lauristons.com
	Chesterton Resdiential	155 Chiswick High Road, Chiswick, London, W4 5TT	020 8747 3133	www.chesterton.co.uk
	Fitz-Gibbon Residential	1 Sutton Court Road, London, W4 4NF	020 8995 3335	www.fitzgibbon.co.uk
	Barnard Marcus	TBC	020 8994 9446	www.sequencehome.co.uk
	Tyser Greenwood	440 Chiswick High Road, Chiswick, London, W4 5TT	020 8994 7022	www.tysergreenwood.co.uk
	Express Property Services	2 Stilehall Parade, Chiswick High Road, London, W4 3AG	020 8994 5000	www.express-property.co.uk
	John Spencer Ltd	388 Chiswick High Road, London, W4 5TF	020 8995 5439	www.johnspencer.co.uk

Area:	Clapham			
Catergory:	A			
Postcode:	SW4			
In Congestion Zone:	No – 2.5 miles outside.			
Parking and Traffic:	Permits & Meters. A205, A3 and roads off Clapham Common get congested.			
Ethnicity Bias:	Afro Caribbean			
Investor Profile:	Pension, Business, Cash&Equity, University			
Crime:	Violence	Sexual	Burglary	Motor
Per 1000 population:	30	2	20	11
Yield Range:	5.1% – 9.0%			

Price Ranges	Low £	Hi £	Low £pw	Hi £pw	Low	Hi
Studio flat	110,000	195,000	170	260	6.9%	8.0%
1 bed flat	160,000	260,000	210	450	6.8%	9.0%
2 bed flat	195,000	360,000	250	500	6.7%	7.2%
2 bed house	310,000	475,000	315	465	5.1%	5.3%
3 bed house	350,000	525,000	360	555	5.3%	5.5%

Valuations above the London average by:	3.9% (£251,170)	
	Actual	**London Average**
Capital growth last 12 months:	–0.7%	19%
Capital growth last 48 months:	57.6%	89%

Tube:	**Clapham Common** Northern Line (Zone 2) – 14 minutes to Charing Cross and 16 minutes to Embankment		
Demand For Letting:	Excellent		
Average void period:	3 days		
Our rating:	**Capital Growth** (out of 5) 3	**Yield** (out of 5) 3	**Total** (out of 10) **6**
Summary:	Popular with the younger generation with strong yields and short voids.		
Sought After Streets:	Clapham High St and all streets off it!		
Description:	I like Clapham. Over the years I have really seen this area smarten itself up. I think it was due to the large green, Clapham Common, attracting everyone in and around surrounding areas to it when the sun came out. As a result a number of cafes, bars and restaurants have popped up and now line the high street.		

Clapham is also relatively unique compared to its other south London areas as it has a direct tube link to the west end – this is why I chose to live here for 3 months. I lived just off the high street which I think is a good place to invest. There is a selection of purpose built and converted flats which all command a good rental and do not stay empty for long. The station is at the end of the high street and the common just beyond that.

If you want to go up-market there is the locally famous Abbeville Village. Famous for its oversized houses, expensive boutiques and speed bumps! Clapham (SW4) has always been considered to be the better alternative to Brixton (SW2). This is still the case but the rise of Brixton has narrowed the gap and people are seeing Brixton as an alternative hence the slight fall in property prices. I think this trend will reverse as Clapham is simply a nicer place to live and the property prices will correct.

Estate Agents:	Name	Address	Tel	Web
	Eagle Properties Ltd	Suite 104, 99–109 Lavender Hill, Clapham, London, SW11 5QL	020 7978 7778	No Website
	Chandlors	100 Clapham High Street, Clapham, London, SW4 7UL	020 7720 6915	www.chandlors .com
	Charles Sinclair & Co	13 Clapham High Street, Clapham, London, SW14 7TS	020 7622 1180	www.charles sinclair.com
	Ludlow Thompson	12 Clapham Road, Clapham, London, SW9 0JD	020 7820 0123	www.ludlow-thompson.co.uk
	Parkside Property Services	22 Clapham Common South Side, Clapham, London, SW4 7AB	020 7498 1000	www.parkside property.co.uk
	Akerwood & Co	6a Old Town, Clapham, London, SW4 0JY	020 7978 2050 New Number 020 867533	www.aker wood.co.uk

▶

Estate Agents:	Name	Address	Tel	Web
	Hugh Henry Ltd	44 Clapham High Street, Clapham, London, SW4 7UR	020 7840 3700	www.hugh henry.co.uk
	Sheraton Law Property Management	1–3 Old Town, Clapham, London, SW4 0JT	08708 444 555	www.sheraton law.com
	Oliver Burn Residential Ltd	362 Clapham Road, Clapham, London, SW9 9AR	020 7622 1121	www.oliver burn.com
	Winkworth Estate Agents	55 Old Town, Clapham Common, Clapham, London, SW4 0JQ	020 7498 8600	www.winkworth .co.uk
Letting Agents:	Name	Address	Tel	Web
	Armitage Residential Lettings	55 Clapham High Street, London, SW4 7TG	020 7498 2243	www.armitage-letts.demon .co.uk
	Vanstons Rentals	45 Balham Hill, London, SW12 9DR	020 8673 9911	www.vanstons .co.uk
	Palace Gate Estates	1 The Polygon, London, SW4 0JE	020 7720 5588	www.palace gateestates .co.uk
	John Hollingsworth	28 Abbeville Road, London, SW4 9NG	020 8675 2224	www.jhollings worth.co.uk
	Hamptons International	27 The Pavement, Clapham, London, SW4 0JE	020 7627 5888	www.hamptons .co.uk
	Adisa-Adesina International	27, Muller Rd London SW4 8BZ	020 8678 7342	No Website

Area:	Covent Garden						
Catergory:	B						
Postcode:	WC2						
In Congestion Zone:	Yes.						
Parking and Traffic:	Permits & Meters. Congested all weekend.						
Ethnicity Bias:	International						
Investor Profile:	Pension, Business, Cash&Equity, University						
Crime:	Violence		Sexual		Burglary		Motor
Per 1000 population:	36		3		10		6
Yield Range:	4.3% – 10.1%						
Price Ranges	Low £	Hi £	Low £pw	Hi £pw	Low	Hi	
Studio flat	135,000	275,000	155	360	6.0%	6.8%	
1 bed flat	225,000	450,000	260	695	6.0%	8.0%	
2 bed flat	350,000	950,000	360	1850	5.3%	10.1%	
2 bed house	475,000	2,000,000	750	2,100	5.5%	8.2%	
3 bed house	650,000	3,000,000	900	2,500	4.3%	7.2%	
Valuations above the London average by:	130.3% (£557,022)						
	Actual			London Average			
Capital growth last 12 months:	5.5%			19%			
Capital growth last 48 months:	6.0%			89%			
Tube:	**Covent Garden** Piccadily (Zone 1) – 7 mins to Oxford Circus						
Demand For Letting:	**Excellent**						
Average void period:	2 days						

	Capital Growth (out of 5)	Yield (out of 5)	Total (out of 10)
Our rating:	4	4	**8**
Summary:	Very central party goer's area with excellent yields and capital growth.		
Sought After Streets:	Everywhere!		
Description:	I would love to have a flat here for all the wrong reasons – its right next to the all night party zones: Leicester Square and Soho. I am not alone in this thinking. The young and very rich 'it' wannabes want to live here also. There is a big premium paid to live here and this is reflected in the high property prices and equally high rental prices. The area has not seen any kind of boom over the last 4 years – its always been expensive!		

	Don't expect to find many properties for sale here. A lot of the buildings in this area have either turned in to retail units or offices. Due to the lack of supply of living space and demand being high the rental figures can ever only be guides. If you have a property that someone wants to rent, and money is no object to them, don't be surprised if you get a yield of 12% or greater. Try to find a property with a unique twist like a balcony overlooking Covent Garden Square for example.			
Estate Agents:	Name	Address	Tel	Web
	Freshwater Group	Freshwater House, 158–162 Shaftesbury Avenue, Covent Garden, London, WC2	020 7836 1555	www.highdorn .co.uk
	Feiner de Smith	47 Poland Street, Covent Garden, London, W1F 7N6	020 7734 3931	www.feiner-desmith.co.uk
	Drury Estates Ltd	2 Nottingham Court, Covent Garden, London, WC2H 9BF	020 7395 5100	www.drury estates.co.uk
	Copping Joyce	196 Shaftesbury Avenue, Covent Garden, London, WC2	020 7379 5300	www.copping joyce.co.uk
	Winkworth	5 New Oxford Street, Covent Garden, London, WC1A 1BH	020 7240 3322	www.wink worth.co.uk
	Alan Croft & Partners	25, Garrick St London WC2E 9AX	020 7240 7494	Number not recognised
Letting Agents:	Name	Address	Tel	Web
	Copping Joyce	196 Shaftesbury Avenue, London, WC2H 8JF	020 7836 2888	www.copping joyce.co.uk
	John D Wood & Co Lettings		020 7436 6666	www.johnd wood.co.uk

▶

Letting Agents:	Name	Address	Tel	Web
	Barnard Marcus		020 7637 8702	www.sequence home.co.uk
	Doorknobs	23, Rose St London WC2E 9EA	020 7240 1716	www.door knobs.co.uk

Area:	**Crouch End**			
Catergory:	C			
Postcode:	N4			
In Congestion Zone:	No – 4.0 miles outside.			
Parking and Traffic:	Permits & Meters. No significant traffic trouble spots.			
Ethnicity Bias:	None			
Investor Profile:	Pension, Business, Cash&Equity,			
Crime:	Violence	Sexual	Burglary	Motor
Per 1000 population:	23	2	17	12
Yield Range:	3.9% – 6.7%			

Price Ranges	Low £	Hi £	Low £pw	Hi £pw	Low	Hi
Studio flat	85,000	135,000	110	160	6.2%	6.7%
1 bed flat	135,000	180,000	140	215	5.4%	6.2%
2 bed flat	160,000	250,000	175	310	5.7%	6.4%
2 bed house	225,000	325,000	170	275	3.9%	4.4%
3 bed house	265,000	475,000	300	465	5.1%	5.9%

Valuations above the London average by:	26.6% (£306,062)	
	Actual	**London Average**
Capital growth last 12 months:	20.7%	19%
Capital growth last 48 months:	75.6%	89%
Tube:	None. 15 min walk to **Finsbury Park** Victoria and Piccadilly Lines (Zone 2) – 6-8 minutes to Kings Cross	
Demand For Letting:	Good	
Average void period:	8 days	

Our rating:	Capital Growth (out of 5)	Yield (out of 5)	Total (out of 10)
	4	2	6

Summary:	Not an easily accessed area but has all the markings to become another Camden.
Sought After Streets:	Coolhurst Rd, Haslemere Rd and St Johns Way.
Description:	Over the last 10 years this place has really come up. I think not having a tube station, ironically, has something to do with it. This has allowed the area to be changed by whoever had the money (as the area was cheap!) – fortunately the people that did have the money changed it in the right way.

▶

There are many converted flats available for the young professional sector as well as the musician/arty type sector and they all mingle well at the many cafes, bars and restaurants in and around The Broadway. I think this area will be the next Camden in the next 10 years. The right people, shops and small businesses are moving in making this one of the areas to be. It is becoming a strong community and this is making it a desirable place to live.

Get in quick to this area. There is a possibility of a train (or even tram) link to be built and at that point the prices will rocket. Over the long term it has one of the best chances of out performing the rest of the market as currently the prices are affordable. For an area to change its perception to outsiders takes a long time. Outsiders perceptions are changing to the positive so I wouldn't hang about.

Estate Agents:	Name	Address	Tel	Web
	Martyn Gerrard Estate Agents	45 The Broadway, Crouch End, London, N8 8DT	020 8348 5135	www.martyn gerrard.co.uk
	Winkworth	12 Broadway Parade, Tottenham Lane, Crouch End, London, N8 9DE	020 8342 9999	www.wink worth.co.uk
	The Property Company	143 Tottenham Lane, Crouch End, London, N8 9BJ	020 8348 8833	www.the-property-company.com
	Prickett & Ellis	134 Crouch Hill, London, N8 9DX	020 8340 8900	www.team prop.co.uk
	Castles Estate Agents	12 Topsfield Parade, Crouch End, London, N8 8PR	020 8348 5515	www.castles-estate agents.co.uk
	Adam Kennedy	8 Wordsworth Parade, Green Lanes, London, N8 0SJ	020 8889 5656	www.adam kennedy.co.uk

▶

Letting Agents:	Name	Address	Tel	Web
	Proton Lettings	70 Grand Parade, Green Lanes, London, N4 1DU	020 8809 2200	No Website
	Hobarts	13 Ferme Park Road, Stroud Green, London, N4 4DS	020 8342 9000	www.hobarts.co.uk
	Alpha-Lets Ltd	371 Green Lanes, London, N4 1DY	020 8809 6144	www.alpha-lets.co.uk
	Noblemere Ltd	549 Green Lanes London N8 0RL	020 8348 4499	No website
	Sunlite Properties Ltd	659 Green Lanes London N8 0QY	020 8245 3620	No Website
	Alexanders Ltd	42 Park Rd Crouch End London N8 8TD	020 8348 5639	No Website

Area:	Ealing					
Catergory:	B					
Postcode:	W5					
In Congestion Zone:	No – 7.0 miles outside.					
Parking and Traffic:	Permits & Meters. Uxbridge Road and the Broadway gets congested.					
Ethnicity Bias:	Asian					
Investor Profile:	Pension, Business, Cash&Equity,					
Crime:	Violence		Sexual		Burglary	Motor
Per 1000 population:	22		1		10	8
Yield Range:	5.6% – 9.0%					
Price Ranges	Low £	Hi £	Low £pw	Hi £pw	Low	Hi
Studio flat	100,000	130,000	135	225	7.0%	9.0%
1 bed flat	140,000	210,000	170	260	6.3%	6.4%
2 bed flat	160,000	300,000	195	375	6.3%	6.5%
2 bed house	195,000	295,000	210	325	5.6%	5.7%
3 bed house	200,000	450,000	280	500	5.8%	7.3%
Valuations above the London average by:	−2.1% (£236,834)					
	Actual			London Average		
Capital growth last 12 months:	28.6%			19%		
Capital growth last 48 months:	111.0%			89%		
Tube:	**Ealing Broadway** District and Central Lines (Zone 3) – 27 minutes to Victoria and 25 minutes to Oxford Circus					
Demand For Letting:	Good					
Average void period:	6 days					
	Capital Growth (out of 5)		Yield (out of 5)		Total (out of 10)	
Our rating:	3		3		6	
Summary:	Potential to find a tenant for life as people rarely move out of the area.					
Sought After Streets:	Byron Rd, Felix Rd and Drayton Green Rd.					
Description:	A fully self contained area. You need not enter Central London for anything but if you wish to it's a 25 minute bus ride to the central border. This I like and so do more and more of the younger generation. The young professional wishing to leave home but wishing to be near their family and friends they grew up with find their home town, Ealing, perfect.					

Ealing is quite a middle class area which is good and is quite suburban – heralded as the queen of the suburbs. The west part of Ealing is considered the cheaper end and this is where you should be looking. This area will eventually rise up as it will be seen as an upmarket alternative to areas such as Southall.

Every shop is here and there are more to come! Ealing is an easy place to get to and I think the retailers know this. It is part of the Hanger Lane Gyratory which links the A406 with the A40. This area is potentially commuterable to Oxford via the A40 or by the excellent rail links offered by Hanwell Train Station. This further attracts tenants wishing to live near London.

Estate Agents:	Name	Address	Tel	Web
	Adams Property Services	22 Northfields Avenue, Ealing, London, W13 9RT	020 8566 3738	www.adams property.co.uk
	Sinton Andrews	8 Springbridge Road, Ealing, London, W5 2AA	020 8566 1990	www.sinton-andrews.co.uk
	Colin Bibra & Co	34 The Mall, Ealing, London, W5 3TJ	020 8567 0077	www.colinbibra.com
	Robertson Smith & Kempson	15 The Mall, Ealing, London, W5 2PJ	020 8840 7677	www.rsk-homes.co.uk
	Russell Collins & Co	102 South Ealing Road, Ealing, London, W5 4QJ	020 8567 7080	www.finda property.co.uk www.ealing homes.co.uk
	Northfields Estates	130 Northfields Avenue, Ealing, London, W13 9RT	020 8840 6666	www.north fields.co.uk
	Tighe Estates	10 Longfield Road, Ealing, London, W5 2DH	020 8579 8601	No Website

▶

Estate Agents:	Name	Address	Tel	Web
	Brendons Estate Agents	Royal Chambers, 104 Pitshanger Lane, Ealing, London, W5 1QX	020 8998 6500	www.brendons .co.uk
	John Martin Estates	82 Pitshanger Lane, Ealing, London, W5 1QX	020 8998 3333	www.john martin estates.com
	Winkworth	5–6 Station Buildings, Ealing Common, Ealing, London, W5 3NU	020 8896 0123	www.wink worth.co.uk
	Grimshaw & Co	5 Station Parade, Ealing Common, London, W5 3LD	020 8992 5661	www.grimshaw homes.co.uk
Letting Agents:	Name	Address	Tel	Web
	Brendons	Royal Chambers, 104 Pitshanger Lane, Ealing, London, W5 1QX	020 8998 6500	www.brendons .co.uk
	Sinton Andrews	8 Springbridge Road, Ealing Broadway, London, W5 2AA	020 8579 9153	www.sinton-andrews.co.uk
	Townends	41 The Broadway, Ealing, London, W5 2NP	020 8579 9282	www.townends .co.uk
	Barnard Marcus		020 8579 5678	www.sequence home.co.uk
	Knight Young & Co	2 Royal Parade, Hanger Lane, London, W5 1ET	020 8991 2987	www.westlondon properties.co.uk

▶

Letting Agents:	Name	Address	Tel	Web
	Ealing Properties	30 Central Chambers, The Broadway, Ealing, London, W5 2NR	020 8840 6898	www.finda property.co.uk
	MBH Property Services	Suite 34, Central Chambers, The Broadway, London, W5 2NR	020 8840 8155	www.mbh homes.co.uk

Area:	East Dulwich			
Catergory:	A			
Postcode:	SE22			
In Congestion Zone:	No – 3.8 miles outside.			
Parking and Traffic:	Free. A205 gets congested as a through route.			
Ethnicity Bias:	Afro Caribbean and African			
Investor Profile:	Pension, Business, Cash&Equity, Retirement.			
Crime:	Violence	Sexual	Burglary	Motor
Per 1000 population:	33	2	14	12
Yield Range:	3.6% – 8.3%			

Price Ranges	Low £	Hi £	Low £pw	Hi £pw	Low	Hi
Studio flat	85,000	160,000	115	145	4.7%	7.0%
1 bed flat	100,000	260,000	160	185	3.7%	8.3%
2 bed flat	135,000	295,000	175	260	4.6%	6.7%
2 bed house	220,000	460,000	240	320	3.6%	5.7%
3 bed house	235,000	500,000	280	360	3.7%	6.2%

Valuations above the London average by:	–8.6% (£221,119)	
	Actual	London Average
Capital growth last 12 months:	30.9%	19%
Capital growth last 48 months:	106.2%	89%

Tube:	None. Train service from **East Dulwich** station (Zone 2) – 11 minutes to London Bridge
Demand For Letting:	Okay
Average void period:	14 days

Our rating:	Capital Growth (out of 5)	Yield (out of 5)	Total (out of 10)
	5	2	7

Summary:	Its going to be connected to the new East London Line tube extension – say no more!
Sought After Streets:	Lordship Lane, Overhill Rd, Abbotswood Rd, Shaw Rd and Burrow Rd.
Description:	Now this is a hotspot! Both East and North Dulwich Train stations will become tube stations on the East London line. Buy anything within a half a mile radius. The prices have not shot up (to factor in the tube additions) as much as I would have thought so real value can be had here. 2006 is the expected year of completion for the tube which is by

▶

no way definite hence investors are putting their money elsewhere for the time being. I would suggest to get in there first.

East Dulwich is not only a hotspot because of the proposed tube stations. If you've ever driven through Dulwich you cannot fail to notice the large greens that surround the whole area – this makes in an excellent place to live and an even better place to invest. Expect rents to rise above the average rate due to the onset of the tube stations.

This place is also school city. Some of the best schools are located here. Expect demand from families as well as commuters.

East Dulwich is the place with the shops. This has led to the development of new houses nearby and they essentially surround the station and these properties are highly sought. There are some flats and I would suggest you buy these due to the area soon to become commuterville.

Estate Agents:	Name	Address	Tel	Web
	Harvey & Wheeler	27 Dulwich Village, Dulwich, London, SE21 7BN	020 8693 4321	www.harvey wheeler.com
	Wates Residential	119 Dulwich Village, Dulwich, London, SE21 7BJ	020 8299 0922	www.spencer kennedy.co.uk
	Dulwich & Village Residential Ltd	397–399 Lordship Lane, Dulwich, London, SE22 8JN	020 8693 4999	www.dulwich andvillage.com
	Spencer Kennedy	1c Carlton Avenue, Dulwich, London, SE21 7DE	020 8693 7835	www.spencer kennedy.co.uk
	Hindwoods Hunter Payne	98 Grove Vale, East Dulwich, London, SE22 8DS	020 8693 2212	www.hhp. property.co.uk
	Durnet Ware & Graves	134–136 Peckham Rye, East Dulwich, London, SE22 9QM	020 8693 4201	www.burnet ware-graves .co.uk

Letting Agents:	Name	Address	Tel	Web
	Voker & Volker		020 8670 8000	www.volkerand volker.co.uk
	Bushells	94 Lordship Lane, Dulwich, London, SE22 8HF	020 8299 6066	www.bushells .com
	Ludlow Thompson	81 Lordship Lane, London, SE22 8EP	020 8299 8300	www.ludlowt hompson.com
	Wates Lettings	119 Dulwich Village, London, SE21 7BJ	020 8299 0922	www.wakes residential.co.uk
	Uniplan	23, Lordship Lane London SE22 8EW	020 8299 2299	www.oak estates.co.uk
	Grove Estates	Melbourne Terrace Melbourne Grove London SE22 8RE	020 8693 9111	No Website

Area:	Elephant & Castle			
Catergory:	A			
Postcode:	SE11, SE17			
In Congestion Zone:	Yes.			
Parking and Traffic:	Permits & Meters. All around the shopping centre gets congested.			
Ethnicity Bias:	Afro Caribbean, African & Asian			
Investor Profile:	Pension, Business, Cash&Equity, University			
Crime:	Violence	Sexual	Burglary	Motor
Per 1000 population:	30	2	20	11
Yield Range:	5.6% – 16.3%			

Price Ranges	Low £	Hi £	Low £pw	Hi £pw	Low	Hi
Studio flat	120,000	220,000	150	295	6.5%	7.0%
1 bed flat	125,000	325,000	210	490	7.8%	8.7%
2 bed flat	170,000	350,000	260	1,100	8.0%	16.3%
2 bed house	185,000	550,000	325	525	5.0%	9.1%
3 bed house	200,000	650,000	440	700	5.6%	11.4%

Valuations above the London average by:	23.4% (£298,400)	
	Actual	London Average
Capital growth last 12 months:	−7.6%	19%
Capital growth last 48 months:	93.2%	89%
Tube:	**Elephant & Castle** Bakerloo and Northern Line (Zone 1) – 15 mins to Oxford Circus	
Demand For Letting:	Good	
Average void period:	5 days	

	Capital Growth (out of 5)	Yield (out of 5)	Total (out of 10)
Our rating:	5	4	9

Summary:	This place is a long term punt but will surely deliver over the long term.
Sought After Streets:	Surrey Square, Chatham Street and Brandon Street.
Description:	I've chosen this area because of the ambitious project planned for completion by 2012. The place will be completely overhauled with the traffic channeled underground and the ugly shopping centre knocked down and replaced with a big glass umbrella housing all the big chains for leisure and retail businesses. There will also be the creation of social and private housing to revamp the area as a whole.

I think the planners have chosen the right area. I've always thought the Elephant was under-priced considering it had the tube (connected to both Bakerloo and Northern Lines), bus connections to all over London and it being only 1 mile or so from the centre of town.

I would stay away from most of the ex-council blocks. The Rockingham Estate is worth a punt as these properties seem of solid construction and could gentrify as from the outside they have a Georgian feel.

Yields will be good and so will capital appreciation in the long term (if you can wait that long!).

Estate Agents:	Name	Address	Tel	Web
	Field & Sons	54 Borough High Street, London, SE1 1XL	020 7407 1375	www.fieldand sons.co.uk
	Daniel Cobb Residential	82–84 Bermondsey Street, London, SE1 3UD	020 7357 0026	www.daniel cobb.co.uk
	Williams Lynch	90 Bermondsey Street, London, SE1 3UB	020 7407 4100	www.williams lynch.co.uk
	Urban Moves Ltd	60 Borough High Street, London, SE1 1XF	020 7378 7892	www.urban moves.com
	Hamptons International	41 Shad Thames, London, SE1 2NJ	020 7407 3172	www.hamptons .co.uk
	Alex Neil	216, Tower Bridge Rd London SE1 2UP	020 7234 0288	www.alex neil.co.uk
Letting Agents:	Name	Address	Tel	Web
	Daniel Cobb Residential	82–84 Bermondsey Street, London, SE1 3UD	020 7357 0026	www.daniel cobb.co.uk
	Hamptons International	41 Shad Thames, London, SE1 2NJ	020 7407 3172	www.hamptons .co.uk
	Stirling Ackroyd Ltd	26 Borough High Street, London, SE1 9QG	020 7940 3888	www.stirling ackroyd.com

Letting Agents:	Name	Address	Tel	Web
	Urban Moves Ltd	60 Borough High Street, London, SE1 1XF	020 7378 7892	www.urban moves.com
	Churchill House Lettings	8 Mill House, London, SE1 2BA	020 8570 3655	www.tower-bridge.co.uk
	County Hall Letting Co	252, Westminster Bridge Rd London SE1 7PD	020 7620 1600	www.county hall.co.uk

Area:	Finchley			
Catergory:	C			
Postcode:	N3			
In Congestion Zone:	No – 7.4 miles outside.			
Parking and Traffic:	Permits & Meters. Free in suburbs. No significant traffic trouble spots.			
Ethnicity Bias:	Japanese			
Investor Profile:	Pension, Business, Cash&Equity, University			
Crime:	Violence	Sexual	Burglary	Motor
Per 1000 population:	14	1	8	4
Yield Range:	5.5% – 7.5%			

Price Ranges	Low £	Hi £	Low £pw	Hi £pw	Low	Hi
Studio flat	90,000	135,000	130	160	6.2%	7.5%
1 bed flat	120,000	165,000	140	210	6.1%	6.6%
2 bed flat	155,000	265,000	180	340	6.0%	6.7%
2 bed house	190,000	260,000	210	335	5.7%	6.7%
3 bed house	235,000	395,000	250	430	5.5%	5.7%

Valuations above the London average by:	−5.0% (£229,662)	
	Actual	London Average
Capital growth last 12 months:	7.9%	19%
Capital growth last 48 months:	60.6%	89%
Tube:	**Finchley Central** Northern Line (Zone 4) – 10 minutes to Euston.	
Demand For Letting:	Good	
Average void period:	9 days	

Our rating:	Capital Growth (out of 5) 3	Yield (out of 5) 3	Total (out of 10) 6
Summary:	Great road, tube and rail links and popular with renters.		
Sought After Streets:	Bedford Rd, Hertford Rd, Huntingdon Rd and Lincoln Rd.		
Description:	I don't particularly like this place and I find it quite drab. So why is it a hotspot? To be more precise it's a 'Hot Stop'. There was an article in the Evening Standard that highlighted this startling fact: The average price of 2–3 bed homes across the 228 tube stops between zones 2–6 were highest on the Northern Line at £270,456. This was a six month survey carried out by the Woolwich. The Finchley area has four tube stations on this line – Finchley Central, East Finchley, West Finchley and Woodside		

▶

Park all within zones 2–6. Now I don't know quite what significance the actual tube line has on a property price (unless the line is notoriously unreliable), but I am happy to include this area as a wildcard entry.

Overlooking the statistical analysis and looking to the fundamentals it has good road links – near the A406, it's 7 miles from the centre, close to Brent Cross Shopping Centre and it's green in places.

There's a lot of investors here (isn't there everywhere?) probably due to the abundance of flats and its proximity to the centre, so you have to act fast if you want to get a piece of the action. Demand is from commuters and young families and always will be. There is nothing to say that demand will not be strong in future due to its 4 tube stops.

Estate Agents:	Name	Address	Tel	Web
	Bennett & Hall Estate Agency	2 Long Lane, Church End, Finchley, London, N3 2PT	020 8346 2208	www.bennett-hall.co.uk
	Moss Kaye Pemberton	22 Northways Parade, Finchley, London, NW3 5EN	020 7724 7442	www.moss kaye.co.uk
	Martyn Gerrard Estate Agents	365 Regents Park Road, Finchley, London, N3 1DE	020 8346 0102	www.martyn garrard.co.uk
	Philip Fisher & Co	3 Dancastle Court, Arcadia Avenue, Finchley, London, N3 2JU	020 8343 3636	No website
	Mann & Co	336 Regents Park Road, Finchley, London, N3 2LN	020 8343 2220	www.right move.co.uk
	Arthur Benabo	7 Ballards Lane, Finchley, London, N3 1UX	020 8346 5911	www.a benabo.co.uk
	Gordon Linke & Co	7 Ballards Lane, Finchley, London, N3 1UX	020 8345 5912	No Website.

Estate Agents:	Name	Address	Tel	Web
	David Harris & Company	358 Regents Park Road, Finchley, London, N3 2LJ	020 8346 9122	www.david harris.co.uk
	Rennick Stark Parntership	266 Regents Park Road, Finchley, London, N3 3HN	020 8371 9977	www.rennick-stark.com
	Jeremy Leaf & Co	863 High Road, Finchley, London, N12 8PT	020 8446 4295	www.jeremy leaf.co.uk
	JAC Strattons	348 Regents Park Road, Finchley, London, N3 2LT	020 8349 5060	www.jac strattons.com
Letting Agents:	**Name**	**Address**	**Tel**	**Web**
	Barnard Marcus		020 8446 0000	www.sequence home.co.uk
	Duchy Lettings Ltd	131 High Street, Barnet, EN5 5UZ	020 8440 4262	www.duchy estates.co.uk
	London-Tokyo Property Services Ltd	351B Regents' Park Road, London, N3 1DH	020 8343 2306	www.london-tokyo.co.uk
	Anscombe & Ringland	338 Regents Park Road, Finchley, London, N3 2LN	020 8349 3320	www.chancellors .co.uk
	Countrywide Residential Lettings Ltd		020 8445 8893	www.right move.co.uk
	David Harris & Co	358 Regent's Park Rd Finchley Central London N3 2LJ	020 8346 9122	www.david harris.co.uk

Area:	Friern Barnet			
Catergory:	C			
Postcode:	N11			
In Congestion Zone:	No – 8.4 miles outside.			
Parking and Traffic:	Free. A406 gets congested.			
Ethnicity Bias:	None			
Investor Profile:	Pension, Business, Cash&Equity & Retirement.			
Crime:	Violence	Sexual	Burglary	Motor
Per 1000 population:	14	1	8	4
Yield Range:	3.6% – 6.7%			

Price Ranges	Low £	Hi £	Low £pw	Hi £pw	Low	Hi
Studio flat	100,000	125,000	110	160	5.7%	6.7%
1 bed flat	130,000	220,000	135	190	4.5%	5.4%
2 bed flat	145,000	350,000	185	290	4.3%	6.6%
2 bed house	200,000	430,000	200	300	3.6%	5.2%
3 bed house	225,000	480,000	260	450	4.9%	6.0%

Valuations above the London average by:	15.0% (£278,174)	
	Actual	**London Average**
Capital growth last 12 months:	25.6%	19%
Capital growth last 48 months:	81.7%	89%
Tube:	**Totteridge & Whetstone** Northern Line (Zone 4) – 34 mins to Tottenham Court Road.	
Demand For Letting:	Good	
Average void period:	8 days	

	Capital Growth (out of 5)	Yield (out of 5)	Total (out of 10)
Our rating:	4	2	**6**

Summary:	You get the best of both worlds – close to the city plus country living.
Sought After Streets:	Friern Barnet Road and Woodhouse Road.
Description:	On the borders of Hertfordshire, it is an easy exit out of London. It's next to the A406 and not too far from the A1 and M1 exits. Flats for sale are readily available and the community is a mixed one – commuters as well as locals. I find this area a safe place to put your money. You have tenant demand from both the young and the old, so you are not relying on one type of tenant. Not as you are if you have a flat in the Docklands where only a city worker would consider living.

The area is next to the very green and very expensive Totteridge. The benefits of this area can be easily accessed as most residents of Friern Barnet are car owners. The tube station listed above is a good 10 minute walk but the area is serviced by New Southgate Station which takes you in to Kings Cross.

Friern Barnet is a much cheaper alternative to Totteridge if you can find the equivalent type of housing – basically large houses. Capital growth will be realized here when everyone is priced out of the surrounding affluent areas.

Estate Agents:	Name	Address	Tel	Web
	Adam Kennedy	10 Queens Parade, Brownlow Road, London, N11 2DN	020 8881 5288	www.adam kennedy.co.uk
	Michael Grove Estate Agents	345 Bowes Road, London, N11 1AA	020 8361 0303	No Website
	Wilkinson Byrne	3 Latham Court, Brownlow Road, London, N11 2ES	020 8365 8900	www.wilkinson byrne.co.uk
	APS Estates	50, Caledonian Rd London N1 9DP	020 7833 5070	www.aps estates.com
	Simon Clarke Residential	130, Ballards Lane London N3 2PA	020 8349 9000 clarke.co.uk	www.simon
	Austin Chambers & Co	191, Woodhouse Rd London N12 9AY	020 8368 6282	www.austin chambers.co.uk

Letting Agents:	Name	Address	Tel	Web
	Anscombe & Ringland	338 Regents Park Road, Finchley, London, N3 2LN	020 8349 3320	www.chancellors .co.uk
	Barnard Marcus		020 8446 0000	www.sequence home.co.uk
	Best Lettings Ltd	73 Friern Barnet Road, London, N11 3EH	020 8361 4303	No website

Area:	**Golders Green**			
Catergory:	B			
Postcode:	NW11			
In Congestion Zone:	No – 5.6 miles outside.			
Parking and Traffic:	Permits & Meters. Free at certain times. No significant traffic trouble spots.			
Ethnicity Bias:	Jewish			
Investor Profile:	Pension, Business, Cash&Equity, University & Retirement.			
Crime:	Violence	Sexual	Burglary	Motor
Per 1000 population:	14	1	8	4
Yield Range:	6.6% – 9.1%			

Price Ranges	Low £	Hi £	Low £pw	Hi £pw	Low	Hi
Studio flat	100,000	150,000	175	220	7.6%	9.1%
1 bed flat	135,000	190,000	195	240	6.6%	7.5%
2 bed flat	200,000	250,000	260	320	6.7%	6.8%
2 bed house	190,000	240,000	310	390	8.5%	8.5%
3 bed house	240,000	420,000	330	550	6.8%	7.2%

Valuations above the London average by:	23.1% (£297,728)	
	Actual	London Average
Capital growth last 12 months:	49.1%	19%
Capital growth last 48 months:	159.4	89%
Tube:	**Golders Green** Northern Line (Zone 3) – 14 minutes to Euston.	
Demand For Letting:	Good	
Average void period:	7 days	

	Capital Growth (out of 5)	Yield (out of 5)	Total (out of 10)
Our rating:	2	3	5

Summary:	Good coverage of tenant groups so voids should be short.
Sought After Streets:	Golders Green Rd, Finchley Rd and Princes Park Avenue.
Description:	My girlfriend used to live here when she was at university and I often stayed over. One thing I liked about this place was that I felt safe no matter what time I went out on to the high road and surrounding streets. This area came 8th out of all the boroughs as the safest place to live which makes this place a comfortable place to live.

▶

The properties are all large. Many of them have undergone conversions into large 2 or 3 bed flats, but there is still a decent amount of family homes to be had. There are a lot of owner occupiers (mainly Jewish and some Japanese) and they will compete as good as the next man to get the property they want.

The area is seen to be the cheaper alternative to areas such as Hampstead as the area is as quiet as its contemporaries. I quite like this area as it is probably one of the best yielding areas out of all the NW postcodes and there is no shortage of demand from all tenant groups – students, young professionals, young families and older families.

It's only 6 miles from the centre, close to the A406 and more significantly close to the A1. This makes this place ideal for people requiring suburban living, proximity to central London and easy access to the northern home counties.

Estate Agents:	Name	Address	Tel	Web
	Ellis & Co	52 Golders Green Road, Golders Green, London, NW11 8LN	020 8455 1014	www.ellisandco.co.uk
	Kingsleys Estate Agents	92 Golders Green Road, Golders Green, London, NW11 8HB	020 8458 3333	www.kingsleys-estates.co.uk
	Winkworth	891 Finchley Road, Golders Green, London, NW11 8RR	020 8458 8313	www.winkworth.co.uk
	Kinleigh Folkard & Hayward	1 Golders Green Rd Golders Green London NW11 8DY	020 8455 1144	www.kfh.co.uk
	Homelink Estates Ltd	21b Accommodation Rd London NW11 8EP	020 8209 1666	No website
	JAC Strattons	48 Golders Green Rd London NW11 8LL	020 8457 8844	www.jacstrattons.co.uk

Letting Agents:	Name	Address	Tel	Web
	Glentree Rentals Ltd	698 Finchley Road, London, NW11 7NE	020 8209 1144	www.glen tree.co.uk
	London-Tokyo Property Services Ltd	351b Regent's Park Road, London, N3 1DH	020 8731 8314	No Website
	Albany Wells	Vero, Russell Gardens London NW11 9NJ	020 8455 1333	www.finda property.co.uk
	Live In London	10 Accommodation Rd London NW11 8ED	020 8209 1414	Under Construction
	Wellington Real Estate	3 Accomodation Rd London NW11 8ED	020 8455 3424	www.wellington realestate.com

Area:	Greenwich			
Catergory:	C			
Postcode:	SE3, SE10			
In Congestion Zone:	No – 5.0 miles outside.			
Parking and Traffic:	Permits & Meters. Greenwich Town Centre gets congested.			
Ethnicity Bias:	None			
Investor Profile:	Pension, Business, Cash&Equity, University			
Crime:	Violence	Sexual	Burglary	Motor
Per 1000 population:	29	2	8	12
Yield Range:	4.1% – 6.4%			

Price Ranges	Low £	Hi £	Low £pw	Hi £pw	Low	Hi
Studio flat	100,000	135,000	120	165	6.2%	6.4%
1 bed flat	135,000	230,000	165	260	5.9%	6.4%
2 bed flat	180,000	450,000	180	425	4.9%	5.2%
2 bed house	210,000	350,000	165	370	4.1%	5.5%
3 bed house	245,000	540,000	290	585	5.6%	6.2%

Valuations above the London average by:	−25.0% (£181,340)	
	Actual	**London Average**
Capital growth last 12 months:	38.4%	19%
Capital growth last 48 months:	96.8%	89%
Tube:	**North Greenwich** Jubilee Line (Zone 3) – 22 mins to Westminster.	
Demand For Letting:	Good	
Average void period:	7 days	

	Capital Growth (out of 5)	Yield (out of 5)	Total (out of 10)
Our rating:	5	2	**7**

Summary:	We have to wait for this one but there are lots of developments. It cannot afford to fail.
Sought After Streets:	Trafalgar Road, Burney Street and Hyde Vale.
Description:	When you think of Greenwich you can only think of one thing – The Millennium Dome. This area, and surrounding areas being the land around the dome, The Greenwich Peninsula and The Millennium Village, will be a hip, futuristic and well connected place to live and work.

▶

The Dome will be an international arena to stage large concerts and corporate events. The land around the Dome will see more homes (around 7,500) and office spaces. There will be hotels, bars, shops, museums – you name it and it will be there. The currently ugly Peninsula is undergoing development for over 9,000 homes. The Village will be a development of nearly 1,500 homes. It has a tube stop and the DLR so it's easy to get north of the river.

Along with this will be the necessary infrastructure and so there will be superstore retail parks, business parks and maybe even a hospital. The area will be a highly desired self servicing town with spectacular river views.

There has been a lot of smart money going into this area. A lot of the new build stuff going to serious investors buying off plan. I would wait for the market to find itself for the next few months. Consider checking it out in the third quarter of 2003.

Estate Agents:	Name	Address	Tel	Web
	Humphreys Skitt & Co	205 Greenwich High Road, Greenwich, London, SE10 8NB	020 8858 1102	www.humphreys-skitt.com
	John Payne	227 Greenwich High Road, Greenwich, London, SE10 8NB	020 8858 9911	www.john payne.com
	Feliks Augustine	5 Greenwich South Street, Greenwich, London, SE10 8NW	020 8858 7111	www.feliks augustine.com
	Meridian Estates Ltd	190, Trafalgar Rd London SE10 9TZ	020 8858 5628	www.meridian estates.co.uk
	Felicity J Lord	27, Greenwich South St Greenwich London SE10 8NT	020 8293 8555	www.tmxfj lord.co.uk
	Oliver Bond Ltd	38, King William Walk London SE10 9HU	020 8858 9393	No Website

Letting Agents:	Name	Address	Tel	Web
	Carlton Property Management Services	161 Trafalgar Road, London, SE10 9TX	020 8305 1889	www.carlton property.co.uk
	Meridian Estates Ltd	190 Trafalgar Road, London, SE10 9TZ	020 8858 5628	www.meridian estates.co.uk
	Hindwoods Hunter Payne Ltd	21 Burney Street, Greenwich, London, SE10 8EX	020 8858 9303	www.hhp-property.co.uk
	Property Liaisons of London Ltd	1a Rotherhithe New Road, Surrey Quays, London, SE16 2AH	020 7252 0111	www.property liaisons.co.uk
	Indigo Property Management	23 Wellington Street, London, SE18 6PQ	020 8317 2002	www.indigo property.com
	Langthorn Ltd	133, Greenwich South St London SE10 8NX	020 8488 1515	No Website

Area:	**Hammersmith**			
Catergory:	B			
Postcode:	W6			
In Congestion Zone:	No – 4.1 miles outside.			
Parking and Traffic:	Permits & Meters. A4 and Hammersmith Bridge gets congested.			
Ethnicity Bias:	None			
Investor Profile:	Pension, Business, Cash&Equity,			
Crime:	Violence	Sexual	Burglary	Motor
Per 1000 population:	26	1	12	7
Yield Range:	4.6% – 9.1%			

Price Ranges	Low £	Hi £	Low £pw	Hi £pw	Low	Hi
Studio flat	100,000	150,000	175	225	7.8%	9.1%
1 bed flat	165,000	265,000	225	410	7.1%	8.0%
2 bed flat	200,000	375,000	300	600	7.8%	8.3%
2 bed house	360,000	465,000	340	455	4.9%	5.1%
3 bed house	375,000	675,000	410	600	4.6%	5.7%

Valuations above the London average by:	14.7% (£277,381)	
	Actual	**London Average**
Capital growth last 12 months:	–2.3%	19%
Capital growth last 48 months:	67.7%	89%
Tube:	**Hammersmith District**, Piccadilly, Hammersmith and City Lines (Zone 2) – 17 mins to Embankment and 11 mins to Paddington	
Demand For Letting:	Good	
Average void period:	6 days	

	Capital Growth (out of 5)	Yield (out of 5)	Total (out of 10)
Our rating:	2	3	5

Summary:	Good yields and tenant demand. You're money is safe here.
Sought After Streets:	Fulham Palace Rd, St Dunstan's Rd and Hammersmith Rd.
Description:	This area is textbook. It's putting theory in to practice. If you build a road, the M4, direct from Heathrow to a London address that is 4 miles from the centre, then watch the big corporations follow. Many a head office is located in Hammersmith, including my own bank, Citibank. This creates strong demand from these workers for good rental properties and this is why it's a hotspot – tenant demand is high!

▶

I have to admit, traffic is bad. Lots of people live here but the road sizes do not reflect this! There is an abundance of flats, both purpose built and conversions, and I would try to go for either flats near the well connected tube station or near the road link M4.

Apart from the traffic I imagine it's a great place to live. Close to the centre of London, lots of trendy bars, restaurants and clubs, good shops and malls and it's next to the river. This area is right next to the BBC headquarters in Shepherds Bush and attracts the higher paid workers to the area as they can afford it.

The fall in prices over the 12 months is simply a correction of the buying frenzy of last year by people desperate to move into the area. Prices are a lot more sensible this year.

Estate Agents:	Name	Address	Tel	Web
	Finlay Brewer	138 Shepherds Bush Road, Hammersmith, London, W6 7PB	020 7371 4171	www.finlay brewer.co.uk
	Wetherby Management Services	274 King Street, Hammersmith, London, W6 0SP	020 8846 9060	www.finda property.co.uk
	Collingwoods	30 Paddenswick Road, Hammersmith, London, W6 0UB	020 8743 8741	No website
	London Estates	61 Dalling Road, Hammersmith, London, W6 0JD	020 8741 8485	www.london-estates.net
	Millar Kitching Management Ltd	Cording House, 34 St James Street, Hammersmith, London, SW1A 1JD	020 7808 3434	www.millar-kitching.co.uk
	Royston	118–120 Glenthorn Road, Hammersmith, London, W6 0LP	020 8563 7100	www.prime location.com
	Cendant – Century 21 UK	Landmark House, Hammersmith Bridge Road, London, W6 9RJ	020 762 6622	www.cendant .com

▶

Letting Agents:	Name	Address	Tel	Web
	Barnard Marcus		020 7603 0000	www.sequence home.co.uk
	Bushells		020 7371 3171	www.bushells .com
	Kinleigh Folkard & Hayward	180 King Street, Hammersmith, London, W6 0RA	020 8563 9889	www.kfh.co.uk
	Marsh & Parsons	107–109 Shepherds Bush Road, London, W6 7LP	020 7605 7760	www.marshand parsons.co.uk
	Sebastian Estates	190 Fulham Palace Road, London, W6 9PA	020 7381 4998	www.sebastian estates.co.uk
	Finlay Brewer Ltd	138 Shepherds Bush Road, London, W6 7PB	020 7371 4171	www.finlay bewer.co.uk

Area:	**Highgate**			
Catergory:	C			
Postcode:	N6, N19			
In Congestion Zone:	No – 4.2 miles outside.			
Parking and Traffic:	Free. Archway Road and Highgate Hill gets congested.			
Ethnicity Bias:	None			
Investor Profile:	Pension, Business, Cash&Equity, University			
Crime:	Violence	Sexual	Burglary	Motor
Per 1000 population:	23	2	17	12
Yield Range:	4.0% – 9.7%			

Price Ranges	Low £	Hi £	Low £pw	Hi £pw	Low	Hi
Studio flat	100,000	140,000	140	260	7.3%	9.7%
1 bed flat	160,000	265,000	185	320	6.0%	6.3%
2 bed flat	185,000	310,000	240	410	6.7%	6.9%
2 bed house	260,000	650,000	300	500	4.0%	6.0%
3 bed house	325,000	840,000	400	650	4.0%	6.4%

Valuations above the London average by:	104.3% (£494,090)	
	Actual	**London Average**
Capital growth last 12 months:	–6.4%	19%
Capital growth last 48 months:	69.8%	89%
Tube:	**Highgate** Northern Line (Zone 3) – 18 mins to Euston and 20 mins to Kings Cross	
Demand For Letting:	Good	
Average void period:	6 days	

	Capital Growth (out of 5)	**Yield** (out of 5)	**Total** (out of 10)
Our rating:	3	3	**6**

Summary:	Expensive but worth it. Long term tenant potential.
Sought After Streets:	Swain's Lane, West Hill Park and Cromwell Avenue.
Description:	You have to look hard here to find something. Highgate is expensive but it's now the alternative to Hampstead and represents good value relative to Hampstead's prices. The area attracts high earners (mandatory to afford these prices!) and they are willing to pay a good rental price for the right property. The yields can be better at the top end of the market as the type of tenants in this area have the money to

▶

pay for a property with the perfect view, plush décor, proximity to the station, location to amenities etc.

I like this area's location considering its neighbour's – Hampstead (mentioned above), Muswell Hill, Crouch End, Islington and Camden. All great areas from a living point of view. If Highgate hasn't got what you want you'll be guaranteed that one of your neighbours has got it. Highgate prides itself for such low migration rates. People moving in Highgate are moving to another place in Highgate.

Estate Agents:	Name	Address	Tel	Web
	Benham & Reeves	35 High Street, Highgate, London, N6 5JT	020 8348 2341	www.benham andreeves.co.uk
	Day Morris Associates	61 Highgate High Street, Highgate, London, N6 5JY	020 8348 8131	www.day morris.co.uk
	Litchfields LTd	44 Highgate High Street, Highgate, London, N6 5JG	020 8348 8000	www.litchfields .com
	Winkworth	36 Highgate High Road, Highgate, London, N6 5JG	020 8341 1988	www.wink worth.co.uk
	Stonebridge & Co	49 Highgate West Hill, Highgate, London, N6 6DA	020 8341 6938	www.stonebridge andco.com
	A Vos Property Agents	West Hill House, 6 Swains Lane, Highgate, London, N6 6QU	020 7267 6600	www.avos property.com
	Simon Clarke Residential	208 Archway Road, Highgate, London, N6 5AX	020 8340 3800	www.simonclarke residential.co.uk

Letting Agents:	Name	Address	Tel	Web
	Mendoza Residential Ltd	16 Aylmer Parade, London, N2 0PE	020 8348 6363	www.mendoza residential.com
	Taylor Gibbs	33 Highgate High Street, Highgate, London, N6 5JT	020 8348 8105	www.taylor gibbs.co.uk
	Anscombe & Ringland	2 South Grove, Highgate Village, London, N6 6BS	020 8340 2600	www.chancellors .co.uk
	Benham & Reeves Residential Lettings	17 Aylmer Parade, Great North Road, London, N2 0PE	020 8341 2335	www.benham reeveslettings .co.uk
	TMD Properties	11, Highgate High St London N6 5JT	020 8341 1166	www.tmd properties.co.uk
	Forestdale Lettings Ltd	196, Archway Rd Highgate London N6 5BB	020 8340 0099	www.ringley .co.uk

Area:	**Holland Park**			
Catergory:	C			
Postcode:	W11, W14			
In Congestion Zone:	No – 4.2 miles outside.			
Parking and Traffic:	Permits & Meters. No significant traffic trouble spots.			
Ethnicity Bias:	None			
Investor Profile:	Pension, Business, Cash&Equity & Retirement.			
Crime:	Violence	Sexual	Burglary	Motor
Per 1000 population:	16	1	10	6
Yield Range:	2.8% – 7.7%			

Price Ranges	Low £	Hi £	Low £pw	Hi £pw	Low	Hi
Studio flat	135,000	360,000	200	360	5.2%	7.7%
1 bed flat	220,000	570,000	320	555	5.1%	7.6%
2 bed flat	325,000	875,000	400	1050	6.2%	6.4%
2 bed house	465,000	1,500,000	520	820	2.8%	5.8%
3 bed house	750,000	2,000,000	720	1900	4.9%	5.0%

Valuations above the London average by:	103.0% (£491,018)	
	Actual	**London Average**
Capital growth last 12 months:	18.6%	19%
Capital growth last 48 months:	60.8%	89%
Tube:	**Holland Park** Central Line (Zone 2) – 11 mins to Oxford Circus.	
Demand For Letting:	Excellent	
Average void period:	3 days	

Our rating:	**Capital Growth** (out of 5)	**Yield** (out of 5)	**Total** (out of 10)
	4	2	6

Summary:	The possibility of improving yields and capital growth. Most sought after location by the rich.
Sought After Streets:	Queensdale Road, Royal Crescent and Portland Road.
Description:	This is one of the most exclusive areas of London. So why is it a hotspot? Well the prices in London are on the way down and the first to fall are at the top end of the market. How far the prices will fall is a matter of debate but properties in Holland Park have fallen and good discounts are to be had here. Thankfully there has been little effect on the rental prices probably due to the high demand from people wishing

▶

to live here. Falling property prices and stable rental prices mean that yields are only going to get better.

The location is superb, probably the best in this book, being between Notting Hill Gate and Kensington; only 3 miles from the centre and connected by the central line – the best tube line to be on (when it works!).

The houses are rarely available and usually get snapped up. You'll have better luck with the flats but be careful of high service charges as many of the buildings are now listed. The converted flats are roomy with high ceilings and good square footage. I don't think it really matters where you buy in Holland Park – as they say 'it's all good'.

Estate Agents:	Name	Address	Tel	Web
	Pereds	Portland House, Portland Road, Holland Park, London, W11 4LA	0207221 1404	www.pereds.com
	David Reynolds	15 Addison Avenue, Holland Park, London, W11 4AQ	020 7602 2422	No website
	John Wilcox & Co	13 Addison Avenue, Holland Park, London, W11 4QS	020 7602 2352	www.finda property.co.uk
	Nina Harris Estate Agents	23 Princedale Road, Holland Park, London, W11 4NW	020 7602 4100	No Website
	Jackson Stops & Staff	14 Portland Road, Holland Park, London, W11 4LA	020 7727 5111	www.jackson-stops.co.uk
	Prompt Estates	8 Addison Avenue, Holland Park, London, W11 4QR	020 7371 1111	www.prompt estates.com

▶

Letting Agents:	Name	Address	Tel	Web
	Cluttons	5 Addison Avenue, Holland Park, London, W11 4QS	020 7371 3600	www.cluttons .com
	Marsh & Parsons	57 Norland Square, London, W11 4QJ	020 7605 6891	www.marshand parsons.co.uk
	Jackson-Stops & Staff	14 Portland Road, Holland Park, London, W11 4LA	020 7727 5222	www.jackson-stops.co.uk
	Prompt Estates Ltd	8 Addison Avenue, Holland Park, London, W11 4QR	020 7371 1111	www.prompt estates.com
	Boulle International	2a, Norland Place London W11 4QG	020 7221 5429	www.boulle .co.uk
	Stewart Walker Associates Ltd	134, Holland Park Avenue London W11 4UE	020 7727 9785	www.finda property.co.uk

Area:	**Islington**			
Catergory:	A			
Postcode:	N1			
In Congestion Zone:	No – 0.4 miles outside.			
Parking and Traffic:	Permits & Meters. Angel and Upper Street gets congested.			
Ethnicity Bias:	None			
Investor Profile:	Pension, Business, Cash&Equity, University			
Crime:	Violence	Sexual	Burglary	Motor
Per 1000 population:	32	2	17	14
Yield Range:	5.2% – 9.2%			

Price Ranges	Low £	Hi £	Low £pw	Hi £pw	Low	Hi
Studio flat	105,000	145,000	185	240	8.6%	9.2%
1 bed flat	120,000	210,000	210	300	7.4%	9.1%
2 bed flat	210,000	325,000	255	465	6.3%	7.4%
2 bed house	320,000	550,000	355	555	5.2%	5.8%
3 bed house	340,000	650,000	450	825	6.6%	6.9%

Valuations above the London average by:	17.7% (£284,573)	
	Actual	**London Average**
Capital growth last 12 months:	13.5%	19%
Capital growth last 48 months:	58.0%	89%
Tube:	**Highbury** and **Islington** Victoria Line (Zone 2) – 8 mins to Kings Cross. Angel Northern Line (Zone1) 3 mins to Euston 10 mins to City.	
Demand For Letting:	Good	
Average void period:	8 days	

	Capital Growth (out of 5)	Yield (out of 5)	Total (out of 10)
Our rating:	4	3	**7**

Summary:	Great place to live – your tenants will appreciate it!
Sought After Streets:	City Road, Essex Road and St Marys Grove.
Description:	One of the first areas to experience gentrification in the 90s. It's now rife with investors and rightly so as there are good yields to be had and there are plenty of new and nearly new developments for sale. Flats are in abundance and two bed flats look the best bet for professional sharers. The one bed flats are good near the Angel for the professionals working in and around the offices that dominate the area.

▶

People want to live here as they can get more for their money. They're coming in from Hampstead, Maida Vale, Camden and even from south of the river. There are plenty of stations to choose from – the two listed above, Caledonian Road, Holloway Road, Drayton Park and the soon to be tube station, Canonbury Rail Station. This has led to the attraction of the area and hence tenant demand is strong. This used to be Tony Blair's home town till he sold up for £565,000 in the mid 90s. It's now worth well over £1m.

The area is well serviced by the usual bars, restaurants and coffee shops, all mainly chains and there just seems to be more and more of them springing up. Islington is firmly on the map and will be for at least another 20 years. It's a safe place to invest but as with all the young professional rented sector – keep abreast of events happening in the city as some of the rented market in Islington will be reliant on it.

Estate Agents:	Name	Address	Tel	Web
	Thomson Currie	313 Upper Street, Islington, London, N1 2XQ	020 7354 5224	www.thomson currie.co.uk
	Drivers & Norris	407–409 Holloway Road, Islington, London, N7 6HP	020 7607 5001	www.drivers .co.uk
	Hotblack Desiato	314 Upper Street, Islington, London, N1 2XQ	020 7226 0160	www.hotblack desiato.co.uk
	Carlton Estate Agents	319 Upper Street, Islington, London, N1 2XQ	020 7359 0000	www.carlton estateagents .co.uk
	Copping Joyce	327–329 Upper Street, Islington, London, N1 2XQ	020 7359 9777	www.copping joyce.co.uk
	Currells Residential	321 Upper Street, Islington, London, N1 2XQ	020 7226 4200	www.currell.com
	Hugh Grover Associates	325 Upper Street, Islington, London, N1 2XQ	020 7226 1010	www.hugh grover.co.uk

▶

Estate Agents:	Name	Address	Tel	Web
	Austin Daniels	268 Upper Street, Islington, London, N1 1RQ	020 7688 0888	www.austin daniels.com
	Warmans	312 St Pauls Road, Islington, London, N1 2LQ	020 7226 2233	www.warmans .co.uk
	Prestige Properties	595 Holloway Road, Islington, London, N19 4DJ	020 7272 6464	www.prestige-properties.net
Letting Agents:	Name	Address	Tel	Web
	Kinleigh Folkard & Hayward	298 Upper Street, Islington, London, N1 2TU	020 7359 3636	www.kfh.co.uk
	Hamptons International	87 Upper Street, London, N1 0NP	020 7359 5675	www.hamptons .co.uk
	Copping Joyce	327–329 Upper Street, London, N1 2XQ	020 7226 4221	www.copping joyce.co.uk
	Evans Baker Lettings	350 Upper Street, London, N1 0PD	020 7226 4994	www.evans baker.co.uk
	The Property Bureau	320 Upper Street, London, N1 2XQ	020 7354 4004	www.theproperty bureau.com
	Currell Lettings Ltd	309 Upper Street, London, N1 2TU	020 7226 9898	www.currell.com

Area:	**Kennington**			
Catergory:	C			
Postcode:	SE11, SE17			
In Congestion Zone:	No – 2.0 miles outside.			
Parking and Traffic:	Permits & Meters. No significant traffic trouble spots.			
Ethnicity Bias:	Afro Caribbean, Portuguese			
Investor Profile:	Pension, Business, Cash&Equity, University			
Crime:	Violence	Sexual	Burglary	Motor
Per 1000 population:	30	2	20	11
Yield Range:	5.1% – 7.5%			

Price Ranges	Low £	Hi £	Low £pw	Hi £pw	Low	Hi
Studio flat	100,000	140,000	145	200	7.4%	7.5%
1 bed flat	135,000	190,000	175	260	6.7%	7.1%
2 bed flat	175,000	325,000	225	375	6.0%	6.7%
2 bed house	255,000	345,000	250	350	5.1%	5.3%
3 bed house	285,000	425,000	300	500	5.5%	6.1%

Valuations above the London average by:	8.2% (£261,746)	
	Actual	**London Average**
Capital growth last 12 months:	–7.6%	19%
Capital growth last 48 months:	93.2%	89%
Tube:	**Kennington** Northern Line (Zone 2) – 10 mins to Embankment.	
Demand For Letting:	Good	
Average void period:	7 days	

	Capital Growth (out of 5)	Yield (out of 5)	Total (out of 10)
Our rating:	4	2	**6**

Summary:	Great location and perfect for above average capital growth.
Sought After Streets:	Kennington Lane, Kennington Road, The Oval.
Description:	This area and surround are a mixed lot – there are beautiful mews dotted around amongst large council blocks and estates so look hard. The reason that I choose Kennington is that it is very close to Westminster – just over Vauxhall Bridge and you're there. Its very popular with professional people (including MPs) seeking a home, rather than a flat to live in. many often seek rented accommodation due to the short term nature of their employment contracts.

My friend has a 2 bed flat in Westminster and he gets £350 a week. He has never had a problem with his tenant and I'm not surprised as this area will only attract quality tenants. Kennington serves Westminster quite well. Look for tenants working north of Vauxhall Bridge as these will tend to be better.

A number of loft apartments are springing up and also converted office blocks overlooking the river. Check out Kennington Cross as this a bit more pleasant on the eye and has a number of converted flats perfect for renters.

Estate Agents:	Name	Address	Tel	Web
	Kinleigh Folkard & Hayward	310–312 Kennington Road, Kennington, London, SE11 4LD	020 7582 7773	www.kfh.co.uk
	Field & Sons	1 Wincott Parade, Kennington Road, London, SE11 6SR	020 7840 0666	www.fieldandsons.co.uk
	Alan Fraser & Co	181–183 Kenington Lane, London, SE11 4EZ	020 7587 1004	No website
	Daniel Cobb	191, Kennington Lane Kennington London SE11 5QS	020 7735 9510	www.danielcobb.co.uk
	Movingspace.com	377–379, Kennington Lane London SE11 5QY	020 7793 1999	www.movingspace.com
	Barnard Marcus	315, Kennington Rd Kennington London SE11 4QE	020 7735 0922	www.sequencehome.co.uk

▶

Letting Agents:	Name	Address	Tel	Web
	Burns & Shield	314 Kennington Road, London, SE11 4LD	020 7582 7799	www.burnsand shield.co.uk
	Daniel Cobb Residential	191 Kennington Lane, Kennington, London, SE11 5QS	020 7735 9510	www.daniel cobb.co.uk
	Greenacre & Co	181 Kennington Lane, London, SE11 4EZ	020 7735 0760	No Website
	Ludlow Thompson	4–6 Clapham Road, London, SW9 0JG	020 7820 4100	www.ludlow thompson.com
	Barnard Marcus		020 7820 3609	www.sequence home.co.uk
	Movingspace. com	377–379, Kennington Lane London SE11 5QY	020 7793 8111	www.moving space.com

Area:	Kensington			
Catergory:	C			
Postcode:	W8			
In Congestion Zone:	No – 3.6 miles outside.			
Parking and Traffic:	Permits & Meters. Kensington Church St & High St gets congested.			
Ethnicity Bias:	International			
Investor Profile:	Pension, Business, Cash&Equity & Retirement.			
Crime:	Violence	Sexual	Burglary	Motor
Per 1000 population:	16	1	10	6
Yield Range:	3.1% – 10.0%			

Price Ranges	Low £	Hi £	Low £pw	Hi £pw	Low	Hi
Studio flat	130,000	350,000	250	350	5.2%	10.0%
1 bed flat	250,000	525,000	265	595	5.5%	5.9%
2 bed flat	295,000	900,000	360	1000	5.8%	6.3%
2 bed house	500,000	1,100,000	390	1100	4.1%	5.2%
3 bed house	750,000	1,700,000	450	2950	3.1%	9.0%

Valuations above the London average by:	190.3% (£702,147)	
	Actual	London Average
Capital growth last 12 months:	–9.6%	19%
Capital growth last 48 months:	159.0%	89%
Tube:	**High St Kensington** Circle, District & Circle Lines (Zone 1) – 15 mins to Oxford Circus	
Demand For Letting:	Excellent	
Average void period:	2 days	

Our rating:	Capital Growth (out of 5)	Yield (out of 5)	Total (out of 10)
	2	3	5

Summary:	It's all good!
Sought After Streets:	Kensington High Street, Queens Gate and Gloucester Road.
Description:	This place is an international address. Famous for Kensington Palace, prices are very expensive. For this hotspot I direct you only to buy the studios and 1 bed flats. Here there are places for sub £300k and you will have no shortage of tenants. There is strong demand from not only UK residents, but also from overseas. I would suggest that you use the services of an agent as they will have the contacts to these overseas tenants who usually pay over the odds.

Service charges on these flats may be high and can sometimes halve your overall profit if you're not careful. I was tempted to purchase a small studio in Kensington High St for £195,000 about 6 months ago yielding around 8% but when looking at the service charges it dropped the yield to 6%.

There are absolutely no no-go spots in Kensington and surrounding the areas so wherever you see something that is cheap – go for it! There are a number of short-leased flats, less than 50 years, that are available. The law is changing with regards to short leases making it possible to renew the lease at the end of the term for a minimal fee. Speak to your solicitor before entering in to this type of market. It's very risky and there are investors out there (very rich ones!) that are playing a game that they can afford to lose.

Estate Agents:	Name	Address	Tel	Web
	Simon Korn	11 Curzon Street, Kensington, London, W1J 5HJ	020 7499 6070	www.simon korn.co.uk
	Shaws Estate Agents Ltd	49 Palliser Road, Kensington, London, W14 9EB	020 7386 9996	www.shaws estateagents .com
	The London & Leicester Property Group	17 Norland Square, Kensington, London, W11 4PX	020 7727 1005	No Website
	Druce & Co	Petersham House, 29 Harrington Road, Kensington, London, SW7 3HQ	020 7581 3771	www.druce.com
	Harpers	53 Abingdon Road, Kensington, London, W8 6AN	020 7938 2311	www.harpers-kensington .co.uk
	Farley & Company Limited	44–48 Old Brompton Road, Kensington, London, SW7 3DY	020 7589 1243	No Website
	F W Gapp	5 Hillgate Street, Kensington, London, W8 7SP	020 7243 0964	www.fwgapp .co.uk

▶

Estate Agents:	Name	Address	Tel	Web
	Leslie Marsh & Co	126 Ladbroke Grove, Kensington, London, W10 5NE	020 7221 0099	www.leslie marsh.co.uk
	Lease of Life Estates	Unit 304 56 Gloucester Road, Kensington, London, SW7 4UB	020 7937 1687	No Website
	Addison Properties	273 Kensington High Street, Kensington, London, W8 6NA	020 7602 6633	www.addisons uk.com
Letting Agents:	**Name**	**Address**	**Tel**	**Web**
	Druce Lamy Ltd	Petersham House, 29 Harrington Road, London, SW7 3HQ	020 7727 7123	www.druce.com
	Knight Frank	54 Kensington Church Street, London, W8 4DB	020 7937 8203	www.knight frank.com
	Lurot Brand Lettings Ltd	5 Kynance Place, London, SW7 4QS	020 7590 2525	www.lurot brand.co.uk
	Scotts (Kensington) Ltd	13b Stratford Road, Kensington, London, W8 6RF	020 7937 9976	www.scotts kensington .co.uk
	Palace Gate	11 Palace Gate, Kensington, London, W8 5LS	020 7581 1631	www.palace gate.com
	Dominics Residential Lettings	38 Gloucester Road, London, SW7 4QT	020 7581 0154	www.dominics uk.com

▶

Letting Agents:	Name	Address	Tel	Web
	Hamptons International	8 Hornton Street, London, W8 4NW	020 7937 9372	www.hamptons .co.uk
	F W Gapp	5 Hillgate Street, London, W8 7SP	020 7243 0964	www.fwgapp .co.uk

Area:	Kilburn			
Catergory:	C			
Postcode:	NW6			
In Congestion Zone:	No – 2.1 miles outside			
Parking and Traffic:	Permits & Meters. Kilburn High Rd gets congested.			
Ethnicity Bias:	Asian, Jewish, Afro Caribbean & Irish			
Investor Profile:	Pension, Business, Cash&Equity, University			
Crime:	Violence	Sexual	Burglary	Motor
Per 1000 population:	27	2	16	11
Yield Range:	5.4% – 8.0%			

Price Ranges	Low £	Hi £	Low £pw	Hi £pw	Low	Hi
Studio flat	110,000	155,000	145	220	6.9%	7.4%
1 bed flat	110,000	210,000	170	250	6.2%	8.0%
2 bed flat	170,000	260,000	210	300	6.0%	6.4%
2 bed house	220,000	300,000	260	325	5.6%	6.1%
3 bed house	300,000	500,000	325	515	5.4%	5.6%

Valuations above the London average by:	19.0% (£287,708)	
	Actual	**London Average**
Capital growth last 12 months:	4.9%	19%
Capital growth last 48 months:	58.6%	89%
Tube:	Kilburn Jubilee Line (Zone 2) – 18 mins to Charing Cross Kilburn Park Bakerloo (Zone 2) – 10 mins to Paddington	
Demand For Letting:	Okay	
Average void period:	14 days	

	Capital Growth (out of 5)	Yield (out of 5)	Total (out of 10)
Our rating:	4	2	**6**

Summary:	Not the prettiest of areas but offers lots of potential growth.
Sought After Streets:	Kilburn High Road, Willesden Lane and Mutrix Road.
Description:	If you head up the Kilburn High Road for 3 miles (leading on to Edgeware Road) you are straight in to Marble Arch. You would never think it as Kilburn High Road and the roads off it are ugly – that's the only word for it. If you look to the right while driving to the centre, you will be looking at West Hampstead as the road is the boundary between Kilburn and West Hampstead. This area is a hotspot as once

the high road eventually 'cleans up' the property prices in this area will be a decent proportion of its neighbours.

The area has great transport links with 2 tube stations and 4 railway stations. This makes this area textbook investing simply because of its location and its not so desirable appearance. It's only a matter of time for this area – how long? it's difficult to tell. One thing I can tell you is that there are a lot of investors purchasing flats in and around Kilburn, especially in the high road area.

You can rely on tenant demand to be strong simply because of its location but there is also a community forming and the high road showing some signs of improvement. People are now choosing to live here rather than seeing it as second best. Give it 10 years and you wont regret investing in this area.

Estate Agents:	Name	Address	Tel	Web
	Harris & Co	106 West End Lane, London, NW6 2LS	020 7624 8101	www.harrisco-property.co.uk
	Temple Trees Estate Agents	201 Belsize Park, London, NW6 4AA	020 7813 0200	www.temple trees.co.uk
	In London Properties	69 Fairfax Road, London, NW6 4EE	020 7625 1266	www.inlondon properties.co.uk
	Greene & Co	146 West End Lane, London, NW6 1SD	020 7328 3232	www.homeis here.co.uk
	Queens Park Real Estates	85, Salusbury Rd London NW6 6NH	020 7372 5950	www.queenspark realestates .co.uk
	Kinleigh Folkard & Hayward	199a, West End Lane West Hampstead London NW6 2LJ	020 7328 2238	www.kfh.co.uk

Letting Agents:	Name	Address	Tel	Web
	Queens Park Real Estates	85 Salusbury Road, London, NW6 6NH	020 7372 5950	www.queenspark realestates .co.uk
	Living Residential	51 Fortune Green Road, London, NW6 1DR	020 7435 6066	www.living residential.com

Letting Agents:	Name	Address	Tel	Web
	Alexanders	Alexander House, 337 West End Lane, London, NW6 1RS	020 7431 0666	www.alexanders-uk.com
	Storm Estates Ltd	31 Mill Lane, London, NW6 1NX	020 7794 8585	www.storm estates.com
	The London Letting Co	190 Kilburn High Road, London, NW6 4JD	020 7624 7976	www.thelondon letting company.com
	Lonafield Property Services Ltd	53 Hemstal Road, London, NW6 2AD	020 7624 6646	No website
	Debben Homes UK Ltd	258 Belsize Road, London, NW6 4BT	020 7316 1860	www.debben homes.co.uk

Area:	Kings Cross			
Catergory:	A			
Postcode:	N1			
In Congestion Zone:	No – 0.1 miles outside.			
Parking and Traffic:	Permits & Meters. No significant traffic trouble spots.			
Ethnicity Bias:	None			
Investor Profile:	Pension, Business, Cash&Equity, University			
Crime:	Violence	Sexual	Burglary	Motor
Per 1000 population:	32	2	17	14
Yield Range:	5.4% – 9.0%			

Price Ranges	Low £	Hi £	Low £pw	Hi £pw	Low	Hi
Studio flat	115,000	185,000	170	255	7.2%	7.7%
1 bed flat	170,000	255,000	230	390	7.0%	8.0%
2 bed flat	190,000	550,000	275	950	7.5%	9.0%
2 bed house	480,000	750,000	500	1100	5.4%	7.6%

Valuations above the London average by:	18.4% (286,409)	
	Actual	London Average
Capital growth last 12 months:	6.8%	19%
Capital growth last 48 months:	92.7%	89%
Tube:	Kings Cross Victoria, Northern, Circle, Metropolitan, Hammersmith & City Lines (Zone 1) – 11 minutes to Oxford Circus. One hour to Heathrow Terminals 1, 2 and 3.	
Demand For Letting:	Okay	
Average void period:	14 days	

	Capital Growth (out of 5)	Yield (out of 5)	Total (out of 10)
Our rating:	4	3	7

Summary:	Not the prettiest or safest area but represents enormous potential considering the inward private and public investment.
Sought After Streets:	Caledonian Rd, St Pancras Rd & Kings Cross Rd.
Description:	Out of all the key station areas in central London like Liverpool St, Euston, Paddington etc, Kings Cross, in my opinion, is the worst area in many aspects – this is why I love it! The area is notorious for its drugs, prostitution and violence but there has been a real effort by the authorites to reduce this. This keeps property prices depressed but ripe to spring up.

▶

There is now a dedicated police station for the area and there is full video surveillance in the worser areas. There is a regeneration programme to start in 2006 and by 2007 the channel tunnel rail link will be functional (hopefully!). So, four years from now, it will be a great place to live hence an above average increase in property prices as the area would have changed.

There is also the Regent Quarter development which will be a development of the original traditional buildings and the building of new homes and commercial units which will attempt to 'clean up' the area. I think this will work. I imagine the illegal trades will move elsewhere and Kings Cross will really come in to fruition by 2010.

The land behind St Pancras and King's Cross stations (formerly known as the railway lands) is set to undergo a major redevelopment. Argent St George have been appointed as the development partners to establish a mixed use scheme that will bring local benefits and help to transform King's Cross into a distinctive urban quarter.

It is hoped the King's Cross Central works will start in 2006 as the Channel Tunnel Rail Link construction works come to a close. Completion is unlikely to be before 2015. Remember – this is a long term bet!

Estate Agents:	Name	Address	Tel	Web
	APS Estates	50 Caledonian Road, London, N1 9DP	020 7833 5070	www.ap estates.com
	Daniel Ford & Co	35 Balfe Street, London, N1 9EB	020 7713 0909	No website

Letting Agents:	Name	Address	Tel	Web
	Hugh Grover Lettings Ltd	Suite 3, Islington Business Centre, Islington High Street, London, N1 9LQ	020 7745 2555	No Website
	The Art of Living (City) Ltd	Second Floor, 9 White Lion Street, London, N1 9PD	020 7833 0003	www.aol-city.com
	Copping Joyce	327/329 Upper Street, London, N1 2XQ	020 7226 4221	www.copping joyce.co.uk
	Frank Harris & Company	104 Southampton Row, London, WC1B 4BL	020 7405 4444	www.frank harris.co.uk
	Black Katz Ltd	22 Baron St, London, N1 9ES	020 7713 7337	www.black-katz.co.uk

Area:	Maida Vale			
Catergory:	C			
Postcode:	W9			
In Congestion Zone:	No – 1.4 miles outside			
Parking and Traffic:	Permits & Meters. No significant traffic trouble spots.			
Ethnicity Bias:	International			
Investor Profile:	Pension, Business, Cash&Equity, University			
Crime:	Violence	Sexual	Burglary	Motor
Per 1000 population:	36	3	10	6
Yield Range:	4.3% – 12.8%			

Price Ranges	Low £	Hi £	Low £pw	Hi £pw	Low	Hi
Studio flat	120,000	220,000	155	320	6.7%	7.6%
1 bed flat	150,000	375,000	220	345	4.8%	7.6%
2 bed flat	220,000	600,000	300	595	5.2%	7.1%
2 bed house	190,000	365,000	350	900	9.6%	12.8%
3 bed house	360,000	1,000,000	400	825	4.3%	5.8%

Valuations above the London average by:	49.6% (£361,708)	
	Actual	**London Average**
Capital growth last 12 months:	22.9%	19%
Capital growth last 48 months:	96.0%	89%

Tube:	**Maida Vale** Bakerloo Line (Zone 2) – 14 minutes to Oxford Circus		
Demand For Letting:	Good		
Average void period:	6 days		
	Capital Growth (out of 5)	Yield (out of 5)	Total (out of 10)
Our rating:	4	3	7
Summary:	Neighbouring areas seeing major investment – it's bound to have a positive effect.		
Sought After Streets:	Clifton Gardens, Warwick Avenue and Sutherland Avenue.		
Description:	Lots to buy here. Many investors are here because of the strong demand for good rental properties. It's a cheaper (but not the cheapest) alternative to St Johns Wood and attracts the better-off professional, say in his/her mid thirties. Corporate lets are not uncommon. Speak to agents in the area about them. Some blue chip companies are looking for nice flats on long leases (up to 5 years in some cases).		

▶

The roads are quite spacious and there are lots of flats for sale. The prices quoted at the bottom end are rare. Most 1 bed flats falling in to the £200k – £300k price bracket. Your money is safe here due to its location. It's right next to the 'oh so expensive' Little Venice, it's near enough to the £500m investment in to Paddington, it's got a great tube link in to Oxford Circus and it's right next to the A40.

Speaking to agents, there is high demand for neutral décor flats with high standard bathrooms and kitchens in Little Venice, which neighbours Maida Vale. Flats are going within hours of them coming on to the rental market.

Estate Agents:	Name	Address	Tel	Web
	Chesterton Residential	26 Clifton Road, Maida Vale, London, W9 1SX	020 7286 4632	www.chesterton .co.uk
	Jones Real Estate Services	6 Randolph Crescent, Maida Vale, London, M9 1DR	020 7266 4821	No website
	Macmillans Estate Agents	44 Formosa Street, Maida Vale, London, W9 2JP	020 7723 3675	www.macmillans london.co.uk
	Vickers & Co	213 Sutherland Avenue, Maida Vale, London, W9 1RU	020 7289 1692	www.prime location.com
	John Barclay Estate Management	389c Harrow Road, Maida Vale, London, W9 3NA	020 8969 3322	www.property world.com
	Pembertons	125 Shirland Road, Maida Vale, London, W9 2EP	020 7266 2020	www. pembertonsltd .com
Letting Agents:	Name	Address	Tel	Web
	Plaza Estates Agency Ltd	Vale House, Maida Vale, London, NW6 5SD	020 7372 6953	www.plaza estates.co.uk
	Pembertons Ltd	125 Shirland Road, Maida Vale, London, W9 2EP	020 7266 2020	www. pembertonsltd .com

Letting Agents:	Name	Address	Tel	Web
	Chesterton Residential	26 Clifton Road, Maida Vale, London, W9 1SX	020 7266 2369	www.chesterton .co.uk
	Sales & Lettings plc	306 Elgin Avenue, London, W9 1JU	020 7266 3355	www.salesand lettingsplc.co.uk
	Cohen & Pride	47 Chippenham Road, London, W9 2AH	020 7266 1406	www.cohenand pride.com
	Ashley Milton Property Services	290 Elgin Avenue, London, W9 1JS	020 7286 6565	www.ashley milton.com
	Martin & Co	4 Delaware Road, Maida Vale, London, W9 2LH	020 7266 5340	www.martinco .com

Area:	Muswell Hill			
Catergory:	C			
Postcode:	N10, N22			
In Congestion Zone:	No – 4.7 miles outside.			
Parking and Traffic:	Free. No significant traffic trouble spots.			
Ethnicity Bias:	None			
Investor Profile:	Pension, Business, Cash&Equity,			
Crime:	Violence	Sexual	Burglary	Motor
Per 1000 population:	23	2	17	12
Yield Range:	3.5% – 7.7%			

Price Ranges	Low £	Hi £	Low £pw	Hi £pw	Low	Hi
Studio flat	110,000	135,000	135	160	6.2%	6.4%
1 bed flat	130,000	175,000	160	260	6.4%	7.7%
2 bed flat	170,000	280,000	210	275	5.1%	6.4%
2 bed house	290,000	400,000	195	310	3.5%	4.0%
3 bed house	300,000	450,000	320	515	5.5%	6.0%

Valuations above the London average by:	15.6% (279,681)	
	Actual	London Average
Capital growth last 12 months:	10.6%	19%
Capital growth last 48 months:	144.7%	89%
Tube:	None. Train service available from Crouch Hill station (Zone 3)	
Demand For Letting:	Good	
Average void period:	7 days	

	Capital Growth (out of 5)	Yield (out of 5)	Total (out of 10)
Our rating:	3	2	**5**

Summary:	A very nice area, good enough to retire to, and good long term tenant potential.
Sought After Streets:	Muswell Hill Road, Leicester Road and Lincoln Road.
Description:	Notice above – there's no tube. This is why it's a hotspot! Why? Well it's like Crouch End (see Crouch End's entry above). Due to the omission of the tube means that it lays kind of undiscovered and keeps the city workers out. The area has a family feel and this is why when people move to Muswell Hill they rarely move. Muswell Hill is a choice not a necessity.

There are more houses than flats which is unusual for London, not many conversions have gone on as would have been expected. This is a safe bet. Expect to have long term tenants, typically families, and a modest return on the investment. Properties in this area are a safe pension and/or a home to retire to.

The area is well serviced for family type residents. Wide roads, plenty of good supermarkets, family orientated pubs and restaurants and leisure facilities for a growing family, such as a cinema, a communal swimming pool and sports complex.

Estate Agents:	Name	Address	Tel	Web
	Prickett & Ellis	114 Alexandra Park Road, Muswell Hill, London, N10 2AH	020 8883 9797	www.team prop.co.uk
	Tatlers	288 Muswell Hill Broadway, Muswell Hill, London, N10 3DU	020 8444 1771	www.tatlers .co.uk
	J H K Homes	336–338 Muswell Hill Broadway, Muswell Hill, London, N10 1DJ	020 8883 5485	No website
	Delemere Properties	418 Muswell Hill Broadway, Muswell Hill, London, N10 1DJ	020 8444 2388	www.delemere-properties.co.uk
	Kinleigh Folkard & Hayward	206, Muswell Hill Broadway Muswell Hill London N10 3SA	020 8883 0123	www.kfh.co.uk
	Keats	500, Muswell Hill Broadway London N10 1BT	020 8365 3426	www.team prop.co.uk
Letting Agents:	Name	Address	Tel	Web
	Kinleigh Folkard & Hayward	206 Muswell Hill Broadway, Muswell Hill, London, N10 3SA	020 8833 2340	www.kfh.co.uk

Letting Agents:	Name	Address	Tel	Web
	C J International Property Agency Ltd	418 Muswell Hill Broadway, London, N10 1DJ	020 8444 9914	www.cj-international.co.uk
	Crayfields Ltd	Lonsto House, 1–3 Princes Lane, London, N10 3LU	020 8444 7757	www.net-lettings.co.uk
	Cromwell Properties	321 Muswell Hill Broadway, London, N10 1BY	020 8883 1888	No website
	Crayfields Ltd	Lonsto House 1–3, Princes Lane London N10 3LU	020 8444 7757	www.net-lettings.co.uk
	D L S Holdings	6, Dukes Avenue Muswell Hill London N10 2PT	020 8444 4389	No website
	Good Homes	335, Muswell Hill Broadway Muswell Hill London N10 1BW	020 8444 7897	No Website

Area:	**Notting Hill**			
Catergory:	C			
Postcode:	W11			
In Congestion Zone:	No – 2.4 miles outside.			
Parking and Traffic:	Permits & Meters. No significant traffic trouble spots.			
Ethnicity Bias:	Afro Caribbean, Spanish & Portuguese			
Investor Profile:	Pension, Business, Cash&Equity, University			
Crime:	Violence	Sexual	Burglary	Motor
Per 1000 population:	16	1	10	6
Yield Range:	3.4% – 6.8%			

Price Ranges	Low £	Hi £	Low £pw	Hi £pw	Low	Hi
Studio flat	140,000	250,000	165	240	5.0%	6.1%
1 bed flat	190,000	460,000	250	460	5.2%	6.8%
2 bed flat	270,000	750,000	325	620	4.3%	6.3%
2 bed house	450,000	950,000	395	615	3.4%	4.6%
3 bed house	500,000	1,200,000	510	985	4.3%	5.3%

Valuations above the London average by:	225.3% (£786,739)	
	Actual	**London Average**
Capital growth last 12 months:	18.6%	19%
Capital growth last 48 months:	60.8%	89%

Tube:	**Notting Hill Gate** Central, Circle and District Lines (Zone 1) – 12 mins to Oxford Circus		
Demand For Letting:	Excellent		
Average void period:	3 days		
	Capital Growth (out of 5)	**Yield** (out of 5)	**Total** (out of 10)
Our rating:	3	2	**5**
Summary:	The famous area that is sought worldwide.		
Sought After Streets:	Kensington Park Road, Ladbroke Road and Clarendon Road.		
Description:	I think we've all seen the film with Hugh Grant. The main thing is that so has the rest of the world! This is an international location. It is the home for the affluent. All the 'riff raff' have been driven out to the North of the area. It's a cosmopolitan place to live with the world famous carnival taking place every year. I would avoid a property on		

▶

the main route of the carnival, as these carnivals have been known to get out of hand in previous years, so I would play it safe.

The area is connected to the right tube line, the central line, and is the choice of anyone working at, or with, the BBC down at White City for those who can afford the rents. It's a very repectable 3 miles from the centre and rich with culture. Prices are not cheap and nor would you expect them to be. The further down the hill, the cheaper it gets. Ex-council flats, I think are good bets. Check out Colville Gardens. This part of Notting Hill is really up and coming (if it hasn't already came!) and is really one of the few places that value can be had.

Estate Agents:	Name	Address	Tel	Web
	McMahon & Co	73 Lansdowne Road, Notting Hill, London, W11 2LG	020 7792 2037	No Website
	Mountgrange Heritage	153 Notting Hill Gate, Notting Hill, London, W11 3LF	020 7221 8921	www.mount grangeheritage .co.uk
	Foxtons	91–95 Notting Hill Gate, Notting Hill, London, W11 3JZ	020 7616 7025	www.foxtons .co.uk
	Barnard Marcus	1 Holland Park Terrace, Portland Road, Notting Hill, London, W11 4ND	020 7221 5455	www.sequence home.co.uk
	Marsh & Parsons	Lime Studios 20, Victoria Gardens London W11 3PE	020 7243 7405	www.marshand parsons.co.uk
	Granvilles	282, Westbourne Park Rd London W11 1EH	020 7229 6776	www.granvilles-london.co.uk
Letting Agents:	Name	Address	Tel	Web
	Anscombe & Ringland	15 Notting Hill Gate, London, W11 3JQ	020 7727 7227	www.chancellors .co.uk

▶

Letting Agents:	Name	Address	Tel	Web
	Knight Frank	298 Westbourne Grove, London, W11 2PS	020 7229 0229	www.knight frank.com
	Tyser Greenwood	123 High Street, Notting Hill, London, W11 3LB	020 7792 9977	www.townends .co.uk
	Leslie Marsh & Co	205 Westbourne Grove, London, W1N 2SB	020 7221 5388	www.leslie marsh.com
	Marsh & Parsons	26 Notting Hill Gate, Bayswater, London, W11 3HY	020 7243 5390	www.marshand parsons.co.uk
	Granvilles	282, Westbourne Park Rd London W11 1EH	020 7229 6776	www.granvilles-london.co.uk

Area:	**Paddington**			
Catergory:	A			
Postcode:	W2			
In Congestion Zone:	No – 0.9 miles outside.			
Parking and Traffic:	Permits & Meters. No significant traffic trouble spots.			
Ethnicity Bias:	None			
Investor Profile:	Pension, Business, Cash&Equity, University			
Crime:	Violence	Sexual	Burglary	Motor
Per 1000 population:	36	3	10	6
Yield Range:	4.6% – 11.4%			

Price Ranges	Low £	Hi £	Low £pw	Hi £pw	Low	Hi
Studio flat	110,000	190,000	160	270	7.4%	7.6%
1 bed flat	155,000	300,000	210	460	7.0%	8.0%
2 bed flat	235,000	500,000	300	1100	6.6%	11.4%
2 bed house	420,000	675,000	410	625	4.8%	5.1%
3 bed house	560,000	1,000,000	500	900	4.6%	4.7%

Valuations above the London average by:	74.7% (£422,560)	
	Actual	London Average
Capital growth last 12 months:	126.6%	19%
Capital growth last 48 months:	191.2%	89%
Tube:	**Paddington**. District, Circle, Bakerloo and Hammersmith & City Lines (Zone 1) – 15 mins to Oxford Circus. Mainline Station to Heathrow in 15 mins and direct line to major areas on M4 corridor.	
Demand For Letting:	Excellent	
Average void period:	3 days	

	Capital Growth (out of 5)	Yield (out of 5)	Total (out of 10)
Our rating:	4	3	7

Summary:	Very affordable! Forget its image and think of its potential.
Sought After Streets:	Edgware Rd, West End Quay, Hermitage St & West End Quay.
Description:	Now this is not the prettiest part of London (bedsit city) and has been considered to be the 'wrong' side of Hyde Park – but this is all about to change. The Paddington Regeneration Partnership are committed to building a new sub-city which will include new bridges and loads of cafes, restaurants and bars. Paddington is now one of central London's

▶

major regeneration opportunities. A number of developments are planned in the area by developers, investment companies and transport interests. In all, it's expected to total 8 million sq ft of built environment, including homes, offices, hotel, retail and leisure developments equivalent in size to Canary Wharf.

Its location is not easily matched. It's right next to the west end, next to the A40 for easy exit from London and a train station that has lines to numerous locations around the UK. Because of its slightly rundown appearance prices are affordable compared to Knightsbridge and Belgravia – and it's highly regarded as the next best thing to Kensington and Notting Hill Gate. I am not alone in this thinking. The development of Paddington Basin has seen large household names locate (or about to locate) their headquarters here.

There is a big housing development planned to be completed by 2005 and an expansion of St Marys hospital which will create an influx of residents and workers which will contribute to the housing demands in the future. There will always be demand for clean 1&2 bed flats from the young professional sector who work in London, as well as people who work at the M4 corridor areas wishing to still live in London.

Estate Agents:	Name	Address	Tel	Web
	Alexander Gordon & Co	1 Craven Terrace, Paddington, London, W2 3QD	020 7402 0070	www.property uk.com
	The London Mews Company Ltd	37–41 Sussex Place, Paddington, London, W2 2TH	020 7402 1146	www.lurotbrand .co.uk
	Alliance Residential	183 Praed Street, Paddington, London, W2 1RH	020 7706 1600	www.alliance residential.co.uk
	Kenwood Estates	23 Spring Street, Paddington, London, W2 1JA	020 7402 3141	www.kenwood-estates.co.uk
	Granvilles	9 Spring Street, Paddington, London, W2 3RA	020 7402 3188	www.granvilles-london.co.uk
	Capital Agencies Ltd	86 Bishops Bridge Rd, London, W2 6BB	020 7727 4000	www.capital .agencies.com

▶

Estate Agents:	Name	Address	Tel	Web
	Compass Real Estate	6 Star St, London, W2 1QD	020 7262 7233	www.compass-re.co.uk

Letting Agents:	Name	Address	Tel	Web
	Behr & Butchoff	105 St John's Wood Terrace, London, NW8 6PL	020 7722 7222	www.behrandbutchoff.com
	Marsh & Parsons	26 Notting Hill Gate, London, W11 3HY	020 7243 5395	www.marshandparsons.co.uk
	Knight Frank	298 Westbourne Grove, London, W11 2PS	020 7229 0229	www.knightfrank.com
	Venus Property Services	175 Queensway, London, W2 5HL	020 7792 4020	No website
	SWO & Co	34a Westbourne Grove, London, W2 5SH	020 7792 8123	www.finderproperty.com
	Go Native Ltd	26, Westbourne Grove London W2 5RH	020 7221 2028	www.gonative.co.uk

Area:	Pimlico			
Catergory:	A			
Postcode:	SW1			
In Congestion Zone:	No – 0.5 miles outside.			
Parking and Traffic:	Permits & Meters. No significant traffic trouble spots.			
Ethnicity Bias:	None			
Investor Profile:	Pension, Business, Cash&Equity, University & Retirement.			
Crime:	Violence	Sexual	Burglary	Motor
Per 1000 population:	36	3	10	6
Yield Range:	5.5% – 8.7%			

Price Ranges	Low £	Hi £	Low £pw	Hi £pw	Low	Hi
Studio flat	125,000	195,000	210	265	7.1%	8.7%
1 bed flat	195,000	360,000	260	425	6.1%	6.9%
2 bed flat	220,000	490,000	325	620	6.6%	7.7%
2 bed house	400,000	650,000	425	905	5.5%	7.2%
3 bed house	475,000	900,000	535	1050	5.9%	6.1%

Valuations above the London average by:	83.7% (£444,317)	
	Actual	London Average
Capital growth last 12 months:	–16.4%	19%
Capital growth last 48 months:	52.0%	89%
Tube:	Pimlico Victoria Lines (Zone 1) – 5 mins to Victoria Station	
Demand For Letting:	Good	
Average void period:	5 days	

	Capital Growth (out of 5)	Yield (out of 5)	Total (out of 10)
Our rating:	4	2	6

Summary:	An unlikely area to offer good yields and good long term capital growth.
Sought After Streets:	Clarendon Street, Vauxhall Bridge Road and Cambridge Street.
Description:	Relatively quiet roads are a great feature of this area. Beautiful large white terraces with pillars line these quiet roads (called stucco terraces). I lived here for 3 months while I was at university and to be honest I didn't really enjoy it much as there was nothing to do – and this is good! The fact that it isn't much fun for a 20 year old university student is a credit to the area. It's so damn quiet and this is why it's popular with affluent, mature renters.

Pimlico is the cheap alternative to Belgravia but it will soon give Belgravia a run for its money. There are many riverside development plans on the Grosvenor Road and surrounding area. It's worth taking a drive and contacting the developers to buy some properties off plan – but be careful, set a yield requirement and get at least a 10% discount on the suggested purchase price.

The rents achieved are strong, hence the yields are okay. I imagine a dip in prices but no crash. As you can see from the figures above they have already dropped by over 16% in the last 12 months. This year it might not be so savage but I do not suspect rental values to fall. Expect to get 9% yield or greater at the latter part of 2003.

Estate Agents:	Name	Address	Tel	Web
	Aldine Honey & Co	25 Eccleston Square, Pimlico, London, SW1V 1NS	020 7834 4901	www.aldine honey.co.uk
	Topcrown Services Limited	71 Cumberland Street, Pimlico, London, SW1V 4ND	020 7931 8895	No website
	Douglas & Gordon	67–68 Warwick Square, Pimlico, London, SW1V 2AR	020 7963 4600	www.douglas andgordon.com
	Dauntons	8, Denbigh St Pimlico London SW1V 2ER	020 7834 8000	www.dauntons .co.uk
	Kinleigh Folkard & Hayward	15, Sussex St Pimlico London SW1V 4RR	020 7821 0001	www.kfh.co.uk
	Halifax Estate Agents	33, Moreton St Pimlico London SW1V 2NZ	020 7834 8340	www.rightmove .co.uk
Letting Agents:	Name	Address	Tel	Web
	Dauntons Residential	8 Denbigh Street, Pimlico, London, SW1V 2ER	020 7834 8000	www.dauntons .co.uk

Letting Agents:	Name	Address	Tel	Web
	Hamptons International	50 Belgrave Road, London, SW1V 1RQ	020 7834 7316	www.hamptons .co.uk
	Douglas & Gordon	67–68 Warwick Square, London, SW1V 2AR	020 7931 8300	www.douglasand gordon.com
	Aldine Honey & Co	25 Eccleston Square, London, SW1V 1NS	020 7834 4901	www.aldine honey.co.uk
	Chesterton Residential		020 7834 9998	www.chesterton .co.uk
	Kinleigh Folkard & Hayward	15 Sussex Street, Pimlico, London, SW1V 4RR	020 7834 3636	www.kfh.co.uk
	Jackson-Stops & Staff	16 Sussex Street, London, SW1V 4RW	020 7931 8300	www.douglasand gordon.com
	Moreton Property Management Services Ltd	72 Rochester Row, London, SW1P 1JU	020 7932 0101	www.moretons .co.uk

Area:	Poplar			
Catergory:	B			
Postcode:	E14			
In Congestion Zone:	No 2.8 miles outside.			
Parking and Traffic:	Permits & Meters. No significant traffic trouble spots.			
Ethnicity Bias:	Afro Caribbean & Asian			
Investor Profile:	Pension, Business, Cash&Equity, University			
Crime:	Violence	Sexual	Burglary	Motor
Per 1000 population:	34	2	10	12
Yield Range:	4.7% – 8.5%			

Price Ranges	Low £	Hi £	Low £pw	Hi £pw	Low	Hi
Studio flat	95,000	120,000	135	175	7.4%	7.6%
1 bed flat	100,000	200,000	160	205	5.3%	8.3%
2 bed flat	125,000	265,000	205	285	5.6%	8.5%
2 bed house	155,000	280,000	210	255	4.7%	7.0%
3 bed house	175,000	230,000	220	280	6.3%	6.5%

Valuations above the London average by:	2.6% (£248,109)	
	Actual	London Average
Capital growth last 12 months:	11.4%	19%
Capital growth last 48 months:	98.0%	89%
Tube:	None. Poplar service available from Docklands Light Railway (Zone 2) – 35 mins to Embankment.	
Demand For Letting:	Okay	
Average void period:	14 days	

	Capital Growth (out of 5)	Yield (out of 5)	Total (out of 10)
Our rating:	2	3	**5**
Summary:	Good yields with the possibility of yields only improving. Lack of transport keep prices low.		
Sought After Streets:	East India Dock Road, Giraud Street and Duff St.		
Description:	I like the 2-bed ex-local authority flats. You will see from above you can get 8.5% yield from these flats which is good for London. Poplar is north of the much talked about Docklands and is linked to the city and Canary Wharf by the DLR system. You get a lot of value in this area as there is no tube and is deemed inferior to the Docklands development.		

▶

There are plenty of developments in Poplar (even more in Docklands!), some council projects and some private developers. It's worth a drive down there to see if you can snap up any off plans in this falling market. There has been a lot of right-to-buys in this area and there are always ex-local authority flats available. You have to be careful of saturation of the rental market in this area. Make sure your property is decorated to a higher standard than the rest as it's a tenant's market and they are proving to be fussier than ever.

Estate Agents:	Name	Address	Tel	Web
	Housemartin Estate Agents	24 Market Way, London, E14 6AH	020 7531 3636	No Website
	Paul James Properties	125 Poplar High Street, London, E14 0AE	020 7093 1032	No website
	F P S Savills	42 Orchard Place, London, E14 0JH	020 7538 1999	No Website

Letting Agents:	Name	Address	Tel	Web
	MCS Meridian Ltd	Grampian House, Meridian Gate, 205 Marsh Wall, London, E14 9YT	020 7538 5388	www.mcs meridian.com
	Spires International	Unit 1, 17 Pepper Street, London, E14 9RP	020 7512 2121	www.spires.co.uk
	Belvoir Lettings Docklands (London)	35 Pepper Street, Docklands, London, E14 9RP	020 7517 6969	www.belvoir lettings.com
	Dauntons	8, Denbigh St Pimlico London SW1V 2ER	020 7834 8000	www.dauntons .co.uk
	Kinleigh Folkard & Hayward	15, Sussex St Pimlico London SW1V 4RR	020 7834 3636	www.kfh.co.uk
	Douglas & Gordon	67–68, Warwick Square London SW1V 2AR	020 7931 8300	www.douglas andgordon.com

Area:	Putney			
Catergory:	A			
Postcode:	SW15			
In Congestion Zone:	No – 4.5 miles outside.			
Parking and Traffic:	Permits & Meters. The High Street gets congested.			
Ethnicity Bias:	None			
Investor Profile:	Pension, Business, Cash&Equity, University			
Crime:	Violence	Sexual	Burglary	Motor
Per 1000 population:	19	1	12	7
Yield Range:	6.3% – 9.4%			

Price Ranges	Low £	Hi £	Low £pw	Hi £pw	Low	Hi
Studio flat	95,000	135,000	155	180	6.9%	8.5%
1 bed flat	140,000	220,000	210	275	6.5%	7.8%
2 bed flat	150,000	325,000	270	425	6.8%	9.4%
2 bed house	200,000	320,000	310	390	6.3%	8.1%
3 bed house	240,000	480,000	385	625	6.8%	8.3%

Valuations above the London average by:	64.9% (£398,732)	
	Actual	**London Average**
Capital growth last 12 months:	47.1%	19%
Capital growth last 48 months:	176.1%	89%
Tube:	**Putney Bridge** District Line (Zones 2/3) – 18 mins to Victoria East Putney District Line (Zones 2/3) – 18 mins to South Kensington	
Demand For Letting:	Good	
Average void period:	6 days	

	Capital Growth (out of 5)	Yield (out of 5)	Total (out of 10)
Our rating:	3	3	**6**

Summary:	Great communications and highly sought after – be prepared to fight for the bargains.
Sought After Streets:	Putney Bridge Road, Brewhouse Street and Upper Richmond Road.
Description:	Just over Putney bridge is Fulham. The place for the rich and famous. Putney offers considerably better value (even though it is still quite expensive) and more choice. There are flats galore, with a respectable amount overlooking the river. The area is well serviced by two tube stations and a railway station.

Prices have soared over the last year, seeing well above average growth – this will not continue! However, there will be modest growth as demand is strong from the richer first time buyers, young families and the dreaded investor! Yields are very respectable for an area that is just over 5 miles from the centre.

Letting agents are crying out for 4–5 bedroomed houses in this area. Premium prices can be charged if you are lucky enough to get one of these properties.

Estate Agents:	Name	Address	Tel	Web
	Cabban & Gaselee Ltd	32 Montserrat Road, Putney, London, SW15 2LA	020 8788 7766	www.cabban .co.uk
	Cousins Realtors	391 Tildesley Road, Putney, London, SW15 3BD	020 8785 3993	No Website
	Allen Briegel	184 Upper Richmond Road, Putney, London, SW15 2SH	020 8780 1642	www.allen briegel.co.uk
	Allan Fuller Estate Agents	149 Upper Richmond Road, Putney, London, SW15 2TX	020 8788 8822	www.finda property.com
	Andrews Estate Agents	170 Putney High Street, Putney, London, SW15 1RS	020 8780 2233	www.andrews .online.uk
	Homestraight	PO Box 19791, Putney, London, SW15 3FE	020 8789 9789	www.home straight.co.uk
	Bairstow Eves	166 Putney High Street, Putney, London, SW15 1RS	020 8780 9995	www.rightmove .co.uk
	James Anderson Estate Agents	78 Low Richmond Road, Putney, London, SW15 1LL	020 8788 6611	www.james anderson.co.uk

Letting Agents:	Name	Address	Tel	Web
	Kinleigh Folkard & Hayward	1 Putney Hill, Putney, London, SW15 6BA	020 8785 3433	www.kfh.co.uk
	Allen Briegel Estate Agents	184 Upper Richmond Road, London, SW15 2SH	020 8780 0900	www.allen briegel.co.uk
	Townends	167 Putney High Street, Putney, London, SW15 1RT	020 8785 4244	www.townends .co.uk
	London-Tokyo Property Services Ltd	176 Putney High Street, London, SW15 1RS	020 8780 1101	www.london-tokyo.co.uk
	Barnard Marcus	210 Upper Richmond Road, Putney, London, SW15 6TE	020 8789 7087	www.sequence home.co.uk
	Lauristons	188 Upper Richmond Road, Putney, London, SW15 2SH	020 8780 8780	www.lauristons .com
	Chesterton Residential	153 Upper Richmond Road, London, SW15 2TX	020 8788 4551	www.chesterton .co.uk
	Andrews Letting & Management	170 Putney High Street, London, SW15 1RS	020 8780 2233	www.andrews online.co.uk
	James Anderson	78 Lower Richmond Road, Putney, London, SW15 1LL	020 8788 6611	www.james anderson.co.uk

Area:	Richmond			
Catergory:	A			
Postcode:	TW9			
In Congestion Zone:	No – 8.8 miles outside.			
Parking and Traffic:	Permits & Meters. Free in suburbs. Upper Richmond Road gets congested.			
Ethnicity Bias:	German			
Investor Profile:	Pension, Business, Cash&Equity & Retirement.			
Crime:	Violence	Sexual	Burglary	Motor
Per 1000 population:	11	1	7	3
Yield Range:	3.9% – 9.0%			

Price Ranges	Low £	Hi £	Low £pw	Hi £pw	Low	Hi
Studio flat	95,000	175,000	165	290	8.6%	9.0%
1 bed flat	165,000	320,000	210	390	6.3%	6.6%
2 bed flat	180,000	500,000	250	795	7.2%	8.3%
2 bed house	240,000	550,000	225	415	3.9%	4.9%
3 bed house	380,000	860,000	325	650	3.9%	4.4%

Valuations above the London average by:	66.7% (£403,203)	
	Actual	London Average
Capital growth last 12 months:	–38.4%	19%
Capital growth last 48 months:	34.9%	89%
Tube:	Richmond District Line (Zone 3) – 30 mins to Embankment.	
Demand For Letting:	Excellent	
Average void period:	3 days	

	Capital Growth (out of 5)	Yield (out of 5)	Total (out of 10)
Our rating:	4	2	**6**

Summary:	Great opportunity to capitalize on fair prices being sought by vendors.
Sought After Streets:	Garrick Close, Kew Road and Ormond Road.
Description:	It's hard to believe that this place is only 8 miles or so from the centre. If you get a property here, then don't expect it to be on the rental market for long – it will get snapped up! The main appeals to this area are its proximity to the M4 corridor companies and accesability to areas such as Devon and Cornwall. The area is well spaced out with plenty of greenery (including Kew Gardens) and is bordered by the River Thames. For this

▶

reason property prices are expensive so do not expect great yields. I estimate that rental prices have to go up – the rental price for a studio is the same as a studio in Leyton and I know where I'd rather live!

You will notice from above there has been a big drop in prices so now is your chance. Basically the prices have corrected themselves from the exorbitant prices being achieved over the last few years. I expect a stabilization of prices for this year with rental figures rising across all property types. Expect yields to get better.

Currently this area has the lowest unemployment rates for London at below 2% and it's hard to find any part of this area undesirable. If there was a fault to this area you would have to look above into the sky – Richmond is under the flight path for the aeroplanes landing at Heathrow. Well you can't have everything! Keep an eye out for the plans for the 5th terminal. This will have a negative impact if it goes ahead, due to the extra noise.

Estate Agents:	Name	Address	Tel	Web
	Foxtons Estate Agents	27a The Quadrant, Richmond, TW9 1DN	020 8973 2700	www.foxtons .co.uk
	Priory Management	16 Kew Green, Kew, Richmond, TW9 3BH	020 8940 4555	www.priory management .com
	Hamptons International	8 The Quadrant, Richmond, TW9 1BP	020 8940 1199	www.hamptons .co.uk
	Featherstone Leigh Ltd	15 Sheen Road, Richmond, RW9 1AD	020 8940 1575	www.feather stoneleigh.co.uk
	Antony Roberts Estate Agents	308 Sandycombe Road, Kew, Richmond, TW9 3NG	020 8940 9401	www.antony roberts.co.uk
	Barnard Marcus	Oriel House 26, The Quadrant Richmond Surrey TW9 1DL	020 8940 6006	www.sequence home.co.uk

Letting Agents:	Name	Address	Tel	Web
	C Howard King & Partners	6 Onslow Road, Richmond, Surrey, TW10 6QF	020 8948 4314	www.howard-king.co.uk
	Tomlinsons Ltd	76 Sheen Road, Richmond, Surrey, TW9 1UF	020 8948 1959	www.tomlinsons lettings.co.uk
	Featherstone-Leigh	1 Royal Parade, Station Approach, Kew, Richmond, Surrey, TW9 3QD	020 8940 7676	www.feather stoneleigh.co.uk
	Priory Management	16 Kew Green, Kew, Richmond, Surrey, TW9 3BH	020 8940 4555	www.priory management .com
	Parkgate Estates (Richmond) Ltd	8 Eton Street, Richmond, Surrey, TW9 1EE	020 8940 2991	www.parkgate-lettings.co.uk
	John D Wood	2 Midmoor House, Key Road, Richmond, TW9 2NQ	020 8940 6611	www.johnd wood.co.uk

Area:	**Shepherds Bush**			
Catergory:	A			
Postcode:	W12			
In Congestion Zone:	No – 4.8 miles outside.			
Parking and Traffic:	Permits & Meters. Shepherds Bush Roundabout & Common gets congested.			
Ethnicity Bias:	International			
Investor Profile:	Pension, Business, Cash&Equity, University			
Crime:	Violence	Sexual	Burglary	Motor
Per 1000 population:	26	1	12	7
Yield Range:	4.5% – 9.5%			

Price Ranges	Low £	Hi £	Low £pw	Hi £pw	Low	Hi
Studio flat	95,000	150,000	150	275	8.2%	9.5%
1 bed flat	120,000	235,000	175	280	6.2%	7.6%
2 bed flat	135,000	320,000	225	310	5.0%	8.7%
2 bed house	190,000	420,000	250	360	4.5%	6.8%
3 bed house	200,000	550,000	325	475	4.5%	8.5%

Valuations above the London average by:	11.6% (£269,900)	
	Actual	**London Average**
Capital growth last 12 months:	21.1%	19%
Capital growth last 48 months:	99.1%	89%
Tube:	**Shepherds Bush** Central Line (Zone 2) – 12 mins to Oxford Circus	
Demand For Letting:	Excellent	
Average void period:	3 days	

Our rating:	Capital Growth (out of 5)	Yield (out of 5)	Total (out of 10)
	4	3	7

Summary:	Good tenant demand and the potential to out perform its neighbours.
Sought After Streets:	Godolphin road, Loftus Road and Sawley Road.
Description:	This is another great location hotspot. It's next to Notting Hill, it has a tube station on the central line that gets you straight in to the centre within 15 mins, it's near to Heathrow and the M4 and is home to the vast BBC centre and studios. Demand to live in this area will be high.

The area seems to be popular with the young arty, media types with studios offering an excellent yield. The area is still a bit drab but there are classier pubs, restaurants and deli's springing up in anticipation of the area coming up.

The area also has three more tube stations on the Hammersmith & City Line being Shepherds Bush, Latimer Road and Goldhawk Road. This has to be a big selling point to any would be renter. If you're looking for a house then you up against the rest of them – this area is flat city.

Estate Agents:	Name	Address	Tel	Web
	Willmotts Estate Agency	75 Goldhawk Road, London, W12 8EH	020 8743 1166	www.willmotts .demon.co.uk
	Century 21 Carlton	109a Uxbridge Road, London, W12 8NL	020 8740 7017	www.century21 carlton.com
	Winkworth	97 Uxbridge Road, Shepherds Bush, London, W12 8NL	020 8749 3394	www.wink worth.co.uk
	Halfapercent.com	5, Cobbold Rd Shepherds Bush London W12 9LA	0871 424 9424	www.halfa percent.com
	Ravenscourt Residential	3, Seven Stars Corner Paddenswick Rd London W12 8ET	020 8740 5678	www.ravenscourt residential.co.uk
	Northfields Estate	127, Askew Rd London W12 9AU	020 8740 8833	www.north fields.co.uk
Letting Agents:	Name	Address	Tel	Web
	Willmotts Estate Agency	75 Goldhawk Road, London, W12 8EH	020 8743 1166	www.willmotts. demon.co.uk
	Homestyle Estate Agents	1 Romney Court, Shepherds Bush Green, London, W12 8PY	020 8740 7172	www.finda property.co.uk
	Bushells	70 Shepherds Bush Road, Hammersmith, W6 7PH	020 7371 3171	www.bushells .com

Area:	**Stepney**			
Catergory:	A			
Postcode:	E1			
In Congestion Zone:	No – 1.9 miles outside.			
Parking and Traffic:	Permits & Meters. No significant traffic trouble spots.			
Ethnicity Bias:	Asian			
Investor Profile:	Pension, Business, Cash&Equity, University			
Crime:	**Violence**	**Sexual**	**Burglary**	**Motor**
Per 1000 population:	34	2	10	12
Yield Range:	6.8% – 8.9%			

Price Ranges	Low £	Hi £	Low £pw	Hi £pw	Low	Hi
Studio flat	100,000	165,000	130	260	6.8%	8.2%
1 bed flat	125,000	195,000	215	310	8.3%	8.9%
2 bed flat	140,000	285,000	240	425	7.8%	8.9%
2 bed house	175,000	300,000	275	415	7.2%	8.2%
3 bed house	200,000	375,000	310	495	6.9%	8.1%

Valuations above the London average by:	−29.5% (£170,406)	
	Actual	**London Average**
Capital growth last 12 months:	10.9%	19%
Capital growth last 48 months:	34.6%	89%
Tube:	**Stepney Green** Hammersmith & City and District Lines (Zone 2) – 22 mins to Embankment.	
Demand For Letting:	Good	
Average void period:	5 days	

	Capital Growth (out of 5)	**Yield** (out of 5)	**Total** (out of 10)
Our rating:	4	3	7

Summary:	Cheap flats can be had here with the strong possibility of capital growth in the short, medium and long term.
Sought After Streets:	White Horse Lane, Louisa Street and Redmans Road.
Description:	The east end in general is the one to watch. It is generally run down with pockets of nice areas. The Docklands has helped to bring up the area as well as the now functioning Canary Wharf.

▶

One thing I like about Stepney is that it's cheap! If you're going to get a bargain in London it's going to be in either Stepney or Poplar (see above). The younger generation working in the city know this. This has helped the mini boom in prices but you can see from the above figures you can still get a yield in excess of 8%.

This area also has mass appeal. It's next to the London Hospital which is also a training hospital and also it's convenient for a lot of the London universities. So as well as tenant demand existing for city workers there is also demand from hospital workers, medics and students.

Estate Agents:	Name	Address	Tel	Web
	Property Liaisons of London Ltd	1 Wapping Wall, London, E1W 3ST	020 7680 0222	www.property liaisons.co.uk
	Atkinson McLeod Ltd	135 Leman Street, London, E1 8EY	020 7488 5555	www.atkinson mcleod.com
	Phoenix Property (UK) Ltd	Gun Court, 70 Wapping Lane, London, E1W 2RL	020 7702 3434	www.phoenix property.co.uk
	FPD Savills	Execution Dock, 80 Wapping High Street, London, E1W 2NE	020 7456 6800	www.fpdsavills .co.uk
	Strettons	41 Artillery Lane, London, E1 7LD	020 7375 1801	www.strettons .co.uk
	Docklands Estates	Lion Court 4 35, The Highway London E1W 3HT	020 7790 7070	www.docklands estates.com
Letting Agents:	Name	Address	Tel	Web
	Atkinson McLeod Ltd	135 Leman Street, London, E1 8EY	020 7488 5555	www.atkinson mcleod.com
	Fell Property Management	115 Ashfield Street, London, E1 3EX	020 7790 4581	www.fell property.co.uk
	Phoenix Property (UK) Ltd	Gun Court, 70 Wapping Lane, London, E1W 2RL	020 7702 3434	www.phoenix property.co.uk

Letting Agents:	Name	Address	Tel	Web
	Property Liaisons of London Ltd	1 Wapping Wall, London, E1W 3ST	020 7680 0222	www.property liaisons.co.uk
	Ananda Residential Lettings	68 Merchant Court, Thorpes Yard London E1W 3SJ	020 7702 2323	www.ananda residential.com
	Capital Dwellings Ltd	47, Fashion St London E1 6PX	020 7375 1515	www.capital dwellings.com

Area:	**Tufnell Park**			
Catergory:	C			
Postcode:	N7, N19			
In Congestion Zone:	No – 2.7 miles outside.			
Parking and Traffic:	Permits & Meters. No significant traffic trouble spots.			
Ethnicity Bias:	None			
Investor Profile:	Pension, Business, Cash&Equity, University			
Crime:	Violence	Sexual	Burglary	Motor
Per 1000 population:	32	2	17	14
Yield Range:	4.2% – 7.9%			

Price Ranges	Low £	Hi £	Low £pw	Hi £pw	Low	Hi
Studio flat	100,000	160,000	125	185	6.0%	6.5%
1 bed flat	125,000	260,000	165	240	4.8%	6.9%
2 bed flat	165,000	370,000	250	330	4.6%	7.9%
2 bed house	220,000	425,000	275	345	4.2%	6.5%
3 bed house	235,000	650,000	330	950	7.6%	7.3%

Valuations above the London average by:	−13.0% (£210,337)	
	Actual	**London Average**
Capital growth last 12 months:	11.9%	19%
Capital growth last 48 months:	59.1%	89%
Tube:	**Tufnell Park** Northern Line (Zone 2) – 13 mins to Euston.	
Demand For Letting:	Good	
Average void period:	9 days	

Our rating:	Capital Growth (out of 5) 4	Yield (out of 5) 2	Total (out of 10) **6**
Summary:	Good long term capital growth potential. The area has good neighbours – it's just a matter of time.		
Sought After Streets:	Tufnell Park Road, Anson Road and Ingestre Road.		
Description:	This is a favourite with the investor. It's in zone 2 on the tube, it has a number of stations down the Kentish Town Road including the Camden Road Station which will soon be turned in to a tube station by 2006 and it's quite near the nicer areas such as Islington, Hampstead, Highgate and Camden. There is a lot of speculative money going in to this and surrounding areas. Investors think that the property prices in		

▶

this area will mirror the prices being achieved by its affluent neighbours.

I like the ex-council properties here. They represent good value and can be easily let out to undergraduate and mature students, families and those seeking an interesting and non-conventional place to live. The area is only 3 miles from the centre and there is plenty to do here. A stroll further up and you hit the colourful Holloway Road. Whatever people say about this road and the roads off it, the properties here are great investments.

If you're looking for a long term punt then this is your one. The yields are not bad, reduced because of the speculation effect, but good enough to be safe. When the properties dry up in the neighbouring areas then the natural choice is Tufnell Park and Kentish Town.

Estate Agents:	Name	Address	Tel	Web
	Drivers & Norris	407 Holloway Road, London, N7 6HP	020 7607 5001	www.drivers .co.uk
	Barnhams Estate Agents	334 Holloway Road, London, N7 6NJ	020 7609 3537	www.barnhams estateagents .com
	Remington Estates (UK) Ltd	221 Holloway Road, London, N7 8HG	020 7697 8800	No website
	Golden Key Commercial Estate Agents	73, Holloway Rd London N7 8JZ	020 7700 2828	www.goldenkey .com
Letting Agents:	Name	Address	Tel	Web
	Drivers & Norris	407 Holloway Road, London, N7 6HP	020 7607 5001	www.drivers .co.uk
	Friar Lettings	212 Hornsey Road, London, N7 7LL	020 7697 8989	No website
	Crestpoly Estates	62 Holloway Road, Holloway, London, N7 8JL	020 7607 7621	No website
	London Accommodation Centre	212 Hornsey Rd, London N7 7LL	020 7700 2834	www.london accommodation centre.com

Letting Agents:	Name	Address	Tel	Web
	Clocktower Workspace – Small Business Letting Agent	Unit 11, Clocktower Workspace, 4 Shearling Way London N7 9TH	No published number.	No Website.

Area:	Wandsworth			
Catergory:	C			
Postcode:	SW18			
In Congestion Zone:	No – 5.4 miles outside.			
Parking and Traffic:	Permits & Meters. A205, A3 and the common gets congested.			
Ethnicity Bias:	None			
Investor Profile:	Pension, Business, Cash&Equity, University & Retirement.			
Crime:	Violence	Sexual	Burglary	Motor
Per 1000 population:	19	1	12	7
Yield Range:	4.2% – 7.5%			

Price Ranges	Low £	Hi £	Low £pw	Hi £pw	Low	Hi
Studio flat	105,000	150,000	130	190	6.4%	6.6%
1 bed flat	125,000	280,000	180	235	4.4%	7.5%
2 bed flat	185,000	400,000	250	325	4.2%	7.0%
2 bed house	195,000	325,000	240	340	5.4%	6.4%
3 bed house	225,000	475,000	325	475	5.2%	7.5%

Valuations above the London average by:	19.0% (£287,791)	
	Actual	London Average
Capital growth last 12 months:	8.1%	19%
Capital growth last 48 months:	86.3%	89%
Tube:	None. Train service from Wandsworth Town (Zone 2) – 12–15 mins to Waterloo	
Demand For Letting:	Good	
Average void period:	5 days	

	Capital Growth (out of 5)	Yield (out of 5)	Total (out of 10)
Our rating:	3	2	**5**

Summary:	A nice place to live – so should attract long term tenants.
Sought After Streets:	Smugglers Way, Northfield Road and Osiers Way.
Description:	This place has really risen up. It has an enviable position being next to the river and has seen loads of industrial buildings converted in to pretty riverside apartments. This trend will continue. The shopping centre has had a revamp and there are more plans to build another shopping/office/housing complex near the town centre.

▶

There is no shortage of properties available to buy, especially new builds, as there are a lot of developments going on at the moment. You won't have much competition from commuters as there is no tube. The area is definitely up-market. Not so up-market neighbouring areas try to cash in on the Wandsworth name – this must tell you something about the area!

What is also great about this area is that you have a choice of Common – Wandsworth or Clapham. Couples that live here grow into families so the potential for a long term tenant is high. The not so brilliant yields are compensated by the likelihood of capital growth. I expect this area to well out perform the market in the long term.

Estate Agents:	Name	Address	Tel	Web
	Nightingale Property Services	165g Nightingale Lane, Wandsworth, London, SW12 8NL	020 8673 5395	No website
	H Rashbrook & Son	91 East Hill, Wandsworth, London, SW18 2QD	020 8874 2211	No website
	Home-london .com	531 Garratt Lane, Wandsworth, London, SW18 4SR	020 8947 6300	www.home-london.com
	Lauristons	188, Upper Richmond Rd London SW15 2SH	020 8780 8780	www.lauristons.com
	Towends Estate Agents	364, Garratt Lane London SW18 4ES	020 8946 7744	www.townends.co.uk
	Barnard Marcus	410 Garratt Lane Earlsfield London SW18 4HW	020 8879 7222	www.sequencehome.co.uk
Letting Agents:	Name	Address	Tel	Web
	Sullivan Thomas & Co Ltd	19 Bellevue Road, Wandsworth Common, London, SW17 7EG	020 8682 3121	www.sullivanthomas.co.uk
	John G Dean	26 Bellevue Road, Wandsworth Common, London, SW17 7EB	020 8767 5121	www.johndean.co.uk

Letting Agents:	Name	Address	Tel	Web
	John D Wood & Co Lettings	501 Battersea Park Road, London, SW11 4LW	020 7223 8848	www.johnd wood.co.uk
	Plum Lettings	130 Brookwood Road, London, SW18 5DD	020 8875 0333	www.plum lettings.co.uk
	Palace Gate Estates	370 Garrett Lane, London, SW18 4ES	020 8877 3444	www.palace estates.co.uk
	Desouza Residential Lettings	173 Garrett Lane, London, SW18 4DP	020 8870 4161	www.desouza residential.co.uk
	Townends Estate Agents	364 Garratt Lane, London, SW18 4ES	020 8946 7744	www.townends .co.uk

Area:	**West Hampstead**			
Catergory:	C			
Postcode:	NW6			
In Congestion Zone:	No – 4.9 miles outside.			
Parking and Traffic:	Permits & Meters. The High Street gets congested.			
Ethnicity Bias:	None			
Investor Profile:	Pension, Business, Cash&Equity, University & Retirement.			
Crime:	Violence	Sexual	Burglary	Motor
Per 1000 population:	27	2	16	11
Yield Range:	5.0% – 8.6%			

Price Ranges	Low £	Hi £	Low £pw	Hi £pw	Low	Hi
Studio flat	130,000	185,000	145	225	5.8%	6.3%
1 bed flat	160,000	275,000	205	345	6.5%	6.7%
2 bed flat	215,000	425,000	240	425	5.2%	5.8%
2 bed house	275,000	420,000	315	440	5.4%	6.0%
3 bed house	375,000	430,000	360	715	5.0%	8.6%

Valuations above the London average by:	31.0% (£316,924)	
	Actual	London Average
Capital growth last 12 months:	4.9%	19%
Capital growth last 48 months:	58.6%	89%
Tube:	West Hampstead Jubilee Line (Zone 2) – 16 mins to Charing Cross	
Demand For Letting:	Excellent	
Average void period:	4 days	

Our rating:	Capital Growth (out of 5)	Yield (out of 5)	Total (out of 10)
	4	2	**6**

Summary:	You've got no problem finding a tenant and expect above average capital growth.
Sought After Streets:	Hillfield Road, Mill Lane and West End Lane.
Description:	Any area with the Hampstead name is bound to do well. It's cheaper than Hampstead itself and better connected than Hampstead Garden Suburb.
	Apart from its main tube station mentioned above it has one other tube station and six mainline stations close by. Therefore the whole wider area is a good bet. There are plenty of flat conversions to be had

▶

and ex-local authority flats that represent good value. The yields again are not the best but the opportunity for capital growth is strong because its Hampstead.

There has been a lot of inward private investment that has attracted commercial and retail enterprises. This has led to major job creation which can only mean good tenant demand. I think rental values will go up in excess of the rate of inflation and the property prices will level off for the year. This will only increase the yield but will still be under the national average.

Estate Agents:	Name	Address	Tel	Web
	William Nelhams & Co	711 Finchley Road, West Hampstead, London, NW2 2JN	020 8458 8044	www.finda property.com
	Brian Lack & Company	249 West End Lane, West Hampstead, London, NW6 1XN	020 7431 5550	www.brianlack .co.uk
	Dutch & Dutch Estate Agents	174 West End Lane, West Hampstead, London, NW6 1SW	020 7794 7788	www.dutchn dutch.co.uk
	Aldergill Limited	118a Cholmley Gardens, West Hampstead, London, NW6 1AA	020 7794 0778	No Website
	Tarrant & Son	108 Mill Lane, West Hampstead, London, NW6 1NF	020 7435 4141	www.finda property.com
	Roger Samuel Residential	173 West End Lane, West Hampstead, London, NW6 2LY	020 7624 4443	www.roger samuel.co.uk
	Greene & Co	146 West End Lane, West Hampstead, London, NW6 1SD	020 7328 3232	www.homeis here.co.uk

▶

Estate Agents:	Name	Address	Tel	Web
	Harris & Co	106 West End Lane, West Hampstead, London, NW6 2LR	020 7624 8101	www.harrisco-property.co.uk
	Havens	47 Mill Lane, West Hampstead, London, NW6 1HB	020 7431 1113	No Website
	The Total Realty Company	158 Fortress Road, West Hampstead, London, NW5 2HR	020 7284 2967	www.total realty.co.uk
Letting Agents:	**Name**	**Address**	**Tel**	**Web**
	FPD Savills plc		020 7472 5000	www.fpdsavills .co.uk
	Hamptons International	21 Heath Street, London, NW3 6TR	020 7431 4462	www.hamptons .co.uk
	Benham & Reeves Residential Lettings	51–53 Heath Street, Hampstead, London, NW3 6UG	020 7435 9681	www.benham reeveslettings .co.uk
	Anscombe & Ringland	55 Heath Street, Hampstead, London, NW3 6UG	020 7794 1151	www.chancellors .co.uk
	Jeffersons Management Services	124 Finchley Road, Hampstead, London, NW3 5HT	020 7794 0091	www.jeffersons .uk.net
	Behr & Butchoff	5 Holly Hill, Hampstead, London, NW3 6QN	020 7431 7222	www.behrand butchoff.com
	Goldschmidt & Howland Property Services Ltd	13a Heath Street, Hampstead, London, NW3 6TP	020 7435 3355	www.g-h.co.uk

Letting Agents:	Name	Address	Tel	Web
	Chesterton Residential	9 Heath Street, Hampstead, London, NW3 6TP	020 7794 1125	www.chesterton .co.uk
	Heathgate	105 Heath Street, Hampstead, London, NW3 6SS	020 7435 3344	www.heathgate .com

Area:	Wimbledon			
Catergory:	A			
Postcode:	SW19, SW20			
In Congestion Zone:	No – 8.3 miles outside.			
Parking and Traffic:	Permits & Meters. Wimbledon Central, Hill & Common all get congested.			
Ethnicity Bias:	None			
Investor Profile:	Pension, Business, Cash&Equity, University & Retirement.			
Crime:	Violence	Sexual	Burglary	Motor
Per 1000 population:	17	1	6	5
Yield Range:	3.4% – 7.9%			

Price Ranges	Low £	Hi £	Low £pw	Hi £pw	Low	Hi
Studio flat	100,000	200,000	150	210	5.5%	7.8%
1 bed flat	125,000	280,000	190	310	5.8%	7.9%
2 bed flat	140,000	540,000	200	350	3.4%	7.4%
2 bed house	225,000	525,000	250	600	5.8%	5.9%
3 bed house	230,000	775,000	350	775	5.2%	7.9%

Valuations above the London average by:	42.4% (£344,390)	
	Actual	**London Average**
Capital growth last 12 months:	19.3%	19%
Capital growth last 48 months:	102.3%	89%
Tube:	**Wimbledon** District Line (Zone 3) – 25 mins to Victoria.	
Demand For Letting:	Good	
Average void period:	6 days	

	Capital Growth (out of 5)	Yield (out of 5)	Total (out of 10)
Our rating:	4	3	7

Summary:	One of my favourites. Internationally known, always demanded and not bad yields – go for it!
Sought After Streets:	Queens Road, Haydons Road and Church Road.
Description:	It's hard to believe this is London. The only thing that reminds you that it's London is the presence of the tube. This is an internationally known place. Famous for its tennis grounds and competition it attracts buyers from all over the world. For the right property you can charge astronomical rent for the two weeks the event is on.

This is another place like East Dulwich – it's an exceptional place to live. You will be competing for properties with locals trading up and down, people wishing to move here and investors from both home and overseas. In other words it's competitive!

8% yields are nearly possible from the studio and 1 bed flats. Again be careful of service charges as they can really damage your wealth. Avoid apartments with fancy gyms or pools. You're not short of greenery in this area. Try to find properties near the station (they will be expensive though) or try Parkside or the Village for cheaper properties, but you will be restricting your tenants to car owners or non commuters.

Speaking to agents, they say that there is a shortage of houses. Landlords are achieving above their advertised rental prices! In Wimbledon, Central apartments are going within hours.

Estate Agents:	Name	Address	Tel	Web
	Courtenays Estate Agents	Hampden House, 76 Durham Road, Wimbledon, London, SW20 0TL	020 8944 1244	www.fish4 homes.co.uk
	Ernle Estates Ltd	47a Wimbledon Hill Road, Wimbledon, London, SW19 7NA	020 8879 7783	www.ernle-estates.com
	Hawes & Co	91 Broadway, Wimbledon, London, SW19 1QE	020 8542 6600	No Website
	Robert Holmes & Co	35 High Street, Wimbledon, London, SW19 5BY	020 8947 9833	www.robert holmes.co.uk
	Fuller Gilbert & Co	316a Worple Road, Wimbledon, London, SW20 8QU	020 8947 4764	www.fuller gilbert.co.uk
	Coombe Residential	356 Coombe Lane, Wimbledon, London, SW20 0RJ	020 8947 9393	www.coombe-residential.co.uk
	Drakesfield	106 Merton High Street, Wimbledon, London, SW19 1BD	020 8715 9444	www.drakes field.co.uk

Estate Agents:	Name	Address	Tel	Web
	Andrew Purnell & Co	3 The Pavement, Worple Road, Wimbledon, London, SW19 4DA	020 8879 7888	www.andrew purnell.co.uk
	C James & Co	141 Kingston Road, Merton Park, Wimbledon, London, SW19 2LJ	020 8542 3232	www.cjames .co.uk

Letting Agents:	Name	Address	Tel	Web
	John D Wood Lettings & Co Ltd	5, Chruch Road, London, SW19 5DW	020 8946 9447	www.johnd wood.co.uk
	Ludlow Thompson	43–45 Wimbledon Hill Road, London, SW19 7NA	020 8405 5432	www.ludlow thompson.com
	Hamptons International	Hampton House, High Street, Wimbledon, London, SW19 5BA	020 8944 1301	www.hamptons .co.uk
	Lords Letting & Property Management	Elizabeth House, 16 Ridgway, Wimbledon, London, SW19 4QN	020 8408 5677	www.lords online.co.uk
	Townchoice	17 Church Road, Wimbledon, London, SW19 5DQ	020 8947 7351	www.town choice.com
	Coombe Residential	356 Coombe Lane, Wimbledon, London, SW20 0RJ	020 8947 5547	www.coombe-residential.co.uk
	Ellisons Letting & Management	1st Floor, 13 Queens Road, Wimbledon, London, SW18 4ES	020 8944 8626	www.ellisons .uk.com

▶

Letting Agents:	Name	Address	Tel	Web
	Lauristons	66–68 Wimbledon Hill Road, Wimbledon, London, SW19 7PA	020 8405 5340	www.lauristons .com
	Kinleigh Folkard & Hayward	149 Arthur Road, Wimbledon, London, SW19 8AB	020 8944 7558	www.kfh.co.uk
	Robert Holmes & Co	Willow House, 35 High Street, Wimbledon Common, London, SW19 5BY	020 8879 9669	www.robert holmes.co.uk

Proposed Tube Stations

There is a psychological factor in being near the tube – you feel connected with the rest of London. Everyone knows that if you have a property near a tube station then your property is not going to remain empty for long and you will be able to sell the property swiftly. So knowing where the next tube stations are going to appear can be a very good for your wealth.

All the following areas are *proposed* tube stations for completion within the next 5 years and therefore I consider them all hotspots. All these areas are Category A hotspots as they will undoubtedly return you a yield and a capital growth above the national average over the long term, if you get in there early enough.

Figure 1

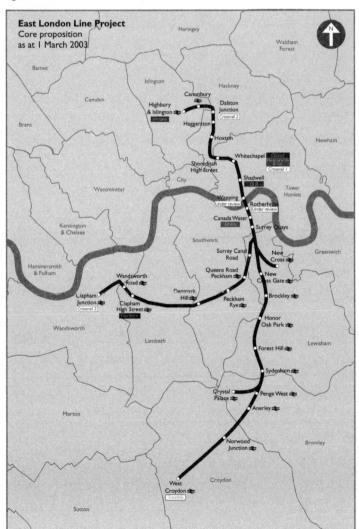

Figure 2

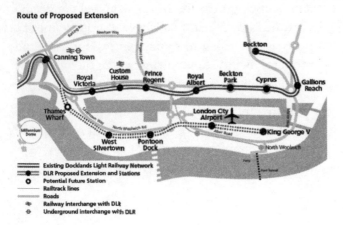

Figure 3

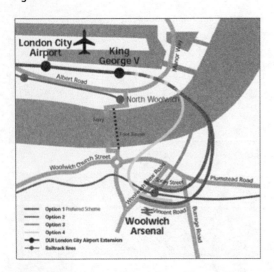

Tube Station	Line	Description
Bishopsgate	East London	In the heart of the city. Unlikely to be many residential opportunities.
Hoxton	East London	Starting to smarten up. Very popular with young professionals and arty media types.
Haggerston	East London	Little known area. Some bargains to be had. A bit shabby though but should all change within 10 years.
Dalston	East London	Bordering Stoke Newington & Islington – this has to be worth a punt!

Tube Station	Line	Description
Canonbury	East London	Next to Islington Green. Pretty location with properties already fairly expensive.
Caledonian Road & Barnsbury	East London	Currently a tucked away little known place but this will really put the place on the (tube) map! Lots of conversions in to flats.
Camden Road	East London	See section on Tufnell Park.
Primrose Hill	East London	Considered a village by some and again is not cheap. Plenty of 1 and 2 bed conversions available.
South Hampstead	East London	The famous Hampsteads – always a safe bet.
Kilburn High Road	East London	Shabby high road thus there will be renovation bargains to be had here.
Brockley	East London	Slowly being discovered. Still affordable. Near Lewisham.
Honor Oak Park	East London	Again, this area is smartening up. Prices start from £75,000 for a studio with yields going up to 10%.
Forest Hill	East London	Cheap flats here. A lot of ex-council flats to be had and newer flats at prices sub £100,000.
Sydenham	East London	A mixture of very nice homes as well as council homes. Considered by many to be an upward moving area. Be quick!
Crystal Palace	East London	Something great is going to replace the burnt out Crystal Palace which will bring fortunes to the area.
Penge West	East London	Great High St and with already good train connections (being Penge East and Penge West).
Anerley	East London	Lots and lots of flats for sale again at sub £100,000 which will mean only good healthy yields.
Norwood Junction	East London	Another place smartening its appearance. Bargain properties to be found if you get in before the full regeneration.
West Croydon	East London	True suburbia. Croydon has that distance to be considered out of London but yet it's going to get a tube. Should be popular with people who already live in Croydon.
Queens Road Peckham	East London	Probably has one of the worst reputations for crime and poverty. This area is for our real risk takers (like me!) where prices are unfairly low and the only way is up.
Peckham Rye	East London	Nicer part of Peckham with more of the older properties here. Choose this part if you're not brave enough to go for Queens Road. £260m going into this place for new low rise blocks, CCTVs and job creation.

Tube Station	Line	Description
East Dulwich	East London	See East Dulwich entry
North Dulwich	East London	See East Dulwich entry
Tulse Hill	East London	Next to (now trendy) Brixton. Very reasonable prices and surprisingly quite picturesque.
Streatham	East London	Real up and coming area over last 3 years due to proximity and affordability. The tube station will only fuel the property prices higher. I suspect the prices will match those of Brixton.
Tooting	East London	Smart pockets of nice properties available. Expect to pay fair prices as demand for properties is high.
Heydon Road	East London	Getting better. No community sense here and high turnover of residents. Should provide cheap properties but be careful of voids prior to the station opening.
Thames Wharf	DLR	A station on the vacant Thames Wharf site will not be constructed as part of the initial scheme because development of the site is restricted by the safeguarding for a potential river crossing. However, the route will allow the opportunity for a station in the future when the site is developed.
West Silvertown	DLR	A station at West Silvertown (between the current entrance to Plaistow Wharf and Knights Road) will serve the existing residential development at Britannia Village and the former Tate & Lyle site known as Peruvian Wharf. A pedestrian crossing will connect the station to the residential area on the north side of the road. The station entrance will be close to local bus stops on North Woolwich Road.
Ponton Dock	DLR	This area is subject to major redevelopment and regeneration, the first phases of which are now complete, including the Barrier Point residential development and new Thames Barrier Park.
London City Airport	DLR	No investment opportunities here. Typical journey time from London City Airport station to Bank will be 22 minutes, Canary Wharf in 14 minutes, and to Stratford via Canning Town in 12 minutes.
King George V	DLR	The station at King George V will be built at ground level to the northern end of Pier Road. This station will be located conveniently for local shops and direct pedestrian links to the ferry/bus terminal at North Woolwich.
Woolwich Arsenal	DLR	Great north-south link. Located on Vincent Road. Check out properties on this road. Should yield a good long term return overall.

Proposed Rail Stations

There are plans to build two railway lines (that flow through existing central tube stations) that link:

1. The East of England to the West of England – CROSSRAIL LINE 1
2. The North East of England with the South West England – CROSSRAIL LINE 2

Completion dates are far off. Expected completion dates are 2012 and 2016 respectively and the final stations are yet to be confirmed. However, I think the plan will go ahead as it is a good idea.

The following areas named below I would consider to be hotspots but do not expect a quick return. If you are thinking of investing in any of these areas focus on getting a strong yield rather than the hope of capital appreciation. The reason for this is that the plans are not definite.

CROSSRAIL LINE 1

Inside Greater London

Crossrail line 1 will create a brand new network of services linking areas to the east and west of London. The heart of the project is the construction of a new tunnelled route across London, with new stations at Liverpool Street, Farringdon, Tottenham Court Road, Bond Street and Paddington. Crossrail Line 1 also includes an option to serve Heathrow Airport. The route will help to regenerate areas such as the Paddington, the Park Royal area, the Lower Lea Valley and the Thames Gateway.

Outside Greater London

Crossrail Line 1 will, for the first time, allow existing suburban rail services to run through London offering a range of possible services to areas such as: Romford and Shenfield to the east, and Ealing and Reading to the west.

Interchanges will be provided with Thames Trains, First Great Western, Chiltern, London Underground, Docklands Light Railway, Thameslink, First Great Eastern, Anglia and possibly Connex services.

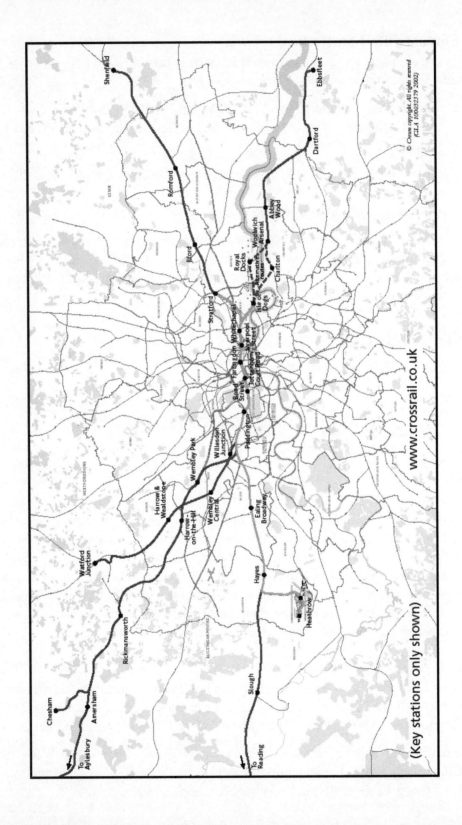

CROSSRAIL LINE 2

Inside Greater London

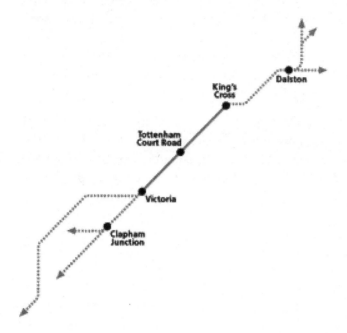

Crossrail line 2 will create a brand new network of services linking areas to the north east and south west of London. The heart of the project is the construction of a core section in tunnel through the centre of London, between Victoria and King's Cross with an interchange with Crossrail line 1 at Tottenham Court Road. new stations at Victoria, Piccadilly Circus, Tottenham Court Road and King's Cross St Pancras. The route will help regenerate areas such as Dalston, Hackney and parts of southwest London.

Outside Greater London

Crossrail line 2 will allow existing northeast and southwest suburban rail services to be linked across London. The plans are yet to be finalized.

Power Of The Postcodes

There is a snobbery element that is unique to London. The postcode sector that the property is in can have an effect on the property price. People sometimes refer to where they live by the postcode as it can sometimes disguise where you actually live! So, for example, if you live in Pimlico your postcode is SW1. If you say you live in SW1 then people think immediately of the grand Buckingham Palace, Downing Street and Belgravia rather than the only slightly up-market Pimlico.

Here is the complete list of all the postcodes in London categorized by the good, the bad and the ugly! This is really a hierarchy of postcodes relative to their neighbours. It means that EC1 (Good) is better than EC3 (Ugly) but it does not mean that W4 (Good) is better than EC3 (Ugly) as they are not neighbours.

Good

E14	Poplar, Isle of Dogs & Docklands
E18	South Woodford
E3	Bow
E4	Chingford
E6	East Ham & Beckton
E8	Hackney
EC1	Clerkenwell
EC2	Moorgate
EC4	Blackfriars
N1	Islington
N10	Muswell Hill
N13	Palmers Green
N14	Southgate
N15	Tottenham (South)
N16	Stoke Newington & Stamford Hill
N2	East Finchley
N20	Totteridge & Whetstone
N21	Winchmore Hill
N3	Finchley
N4	Crouch End, Stroud Green & Finsbury Park
N5	Highbury
N6	Highgate
N7	Holloway, Tufnell Park & Highbury
N8	Hornsey
NW1	Camden Town

NW11	Golders Green	
NW2	Cricklewood	
NW3	Hampstead	
NW4	Hendon	
NW5	Kentish Town	
NW6	West Hampstead	
NW8	St Johns Wood	
SE10	Greenwich	
SE12	Lee & Grove Park	
SE13	Lewisham	
SE21	West Dulwich	
SE22	East Dulwich	
SE23	Forest Hill	
SE24	Herne Hill	
SE3	Blackheath	
SW1	Victoria	
SW10	West Brompton	
SW11	Battersea	
SW13	Barnes	
SW15	Putney	
SW17	Tooting	
SW18	Wandsworth	
SW19	Wimbledon	
SW3	Chelsea	
SW4	Clapham	
SW5	Earls Court	
SW6	Fulham	
SW7	South Kensington	
W13	West Ealing	
W14	West Kensington	
W1	Mayfair & Oxford St	
W11	Notting Hill & Holland Park	
W4	Chiswick	
W5	Ealing	
W6	Hammersmith	
W8	Kensington	
W9	Maida Vale	

Bad

E1	Whitechapel & Stepney
E2	Bethnal Green
E9	Homerton
E12	Manor Park
E13	Plaistow
E16	Silvertown & Canning Town
E17	Walthamstow
N11	New Southgate
N12	North Finchley
N22	Wood Green
NW7	Mill Hill
NW9	Hendon, Colindale & Kingsbury
SE1	Southwark & Bermondsey
SE4	Brockley
SE5	Camberwell
SE6	Catford
SE8	Deptford
SE11	Kennington
SE14	New Cross
SE15	Peckham
SE16	Rotherhithe
SE17	Walworth
SE18	Woolwich
SE26	Sydenham
SE27	West Norwood
SW8	South Lambeth
SW9	Stockwell
SW12	Balham
SW16	Streatham
W12	Shepherds Bush
W2	Paddington
WC1	Bloomsbury
WC2	Covent Garden

Ugly

E10	Leyton
E11	Leytonstone
E15	Stratford
E5	Clapton
E7	Forest Gate
EC3	Fenchurch
N17	Tottenham
N18	Edmonton & Upper Edmonton
N19	Archway
N4	Finsbury Park
N9	Lower Edmonton
NW10	Willesden
SE19	Norwood
SE2	Abbey Wood
SE20	Anerley & Penge
SE24	Herne Hill
SE25	South Norwood
SE28	Thamesmead
SE7	Charlton
SE9	Eltham
SW14	Mortlake
SW2	Brixton
SW20	West Wimbledon
W10	North Kensington
W14	West Kensington
W3	Acton
W7	Hanwell

Congestion Zone

At a glance

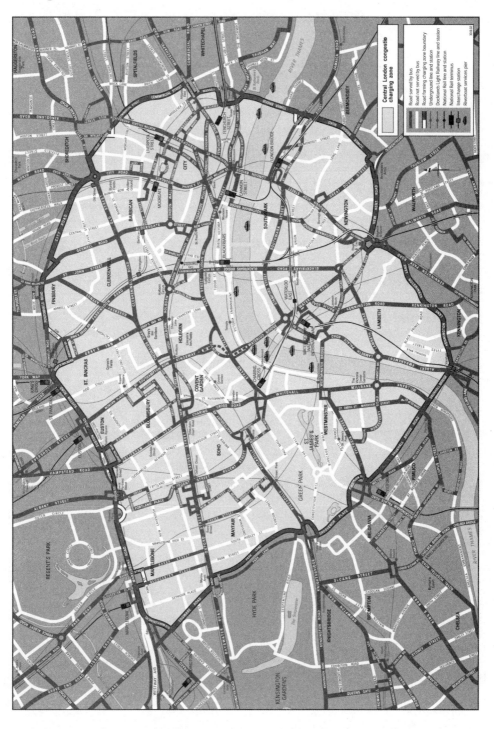

Operating Times: 7.00am to 6.30pm, Monday to Friday, excluding public Holidays

Cost: £5 per day

Exemptions: Disabled people, drivers of alternative fuel vehicles, vehicles with 9 or more seats and drivers of roadside recovery vehicles.

Discounts: 90% for residents if applying for 5 consecutive days or more only.

Penalties: £40 if paid within 14 days
£80 if paid within 28 days
£120 if paid after 28 days

Effect on Property Values

The scheme is relatively new. It has only been in effect for 2 weeks at the time of writing. However, the effect on property values is quite simple once you categorise the properties in to one of these three groups:

Group	Effect	Reasons
Inside the congestion zone	Positive	You are entitled to a large discount, 90%, of the charge which makes living in the zone very cost effective. The actual benefit would be the savings being 90% x 252days x £5 = £1,134 per year. I would say that people may expect to benefit for a period of 10 – 20 years thus equating to £10,000 to £20,000. I imagine that people will over estimate these savings and we may see prices go up by up to £30,000 assuming all other things remain equal. In the future the savings may be greater as Ken Livingstone considers doubling the charge to £10. Also, if this congestion charging works, the roads will be a lot clearer hence making it easier to get to places within the zone.
0 – 3 miles outside the congestion zone	Negative	I say 0 – 3 miles but it could be 5 miles or it could be 1 mile. It will be clearer once the charge settles in. However, one thing is clear – traffic will be worse around the perimeter of the zone. The perimeter will become an unofficial ring road for drivers wishing to get from one side of London to the other without paying the charge. This is bound to make these areas undesirable. Also, it is likely that if you live in the perimeter there is something within the congestion zone that you need to visit – doctors, friends, shops or even a parking space! I wonder how many people are going to pay £5 each time for all these eventualities.

Group	Effect	Reasons
Greater than 3 miles outside the congestion zone	No effect	There will be a safe distance from the congestion zone so that it will not even matter. It may vary in distance depending on where in greater London the location is. But the principle is this – it has to be an area thus is sufficiently self-contained so that there is no reason to go in to the centre during the day.

My Tip

I will be looking at properties just *outside* the zone to see if there are any bargains to be had. As the scheme is new and people generally tend to panic, there may be some vendors over estimating the effect of congestion charging and offering a generous discount on their property. There is also the point that the congestion zone may expand to include the areas that are just out of the zone.

Sign Up For The Property Hotspot Newsletter

So you want to be ahead of the pack. You can subscribe to the Hotspot Newsletter that will be mailed to you first class every quarter and it will detail:

- A detailed and statistical analysis of trends for 10 identified hotspots by the authors.

- The best buy-to-let mortgage deals available on the market.

- Changes in the law affecting the property market.

- Significant news and developments in the property market.

The cost is £19.95 per quarter. You can subscribe to this 'hot off the press' newsletter by faxing, emailing, writing or phoning How To Books and quoting your credit card number or sending a completed standing order form below to:

How To Books Ltd
Head Office
3 Newtec Place
Magdalen Road
Oxford
OX4 1RE
UK

Tel: +44 (0)1865 793806
Fax: +44 (0)1865 248780
Email: info@howtobooks.co.uk
Web: www.howtobooks.co.uk
or visit www.propertyhotspots.net

STANDING ORDER SET UP

PAYER:

Name:	
Bank Branch:	
Address:	
A/C Number:	
Sort Code:	

PAYEE:

Name:	How To Books
Bank Branch:	
A/C Number:	
Sort Code:	

PAYMENT DETAILS:

Amount:	£19.95
Transfer Date (leave blank):	
Repeat:	Every Quarter (3 months)
Last Transfer Date:	To be notified in writing

Please could you set up the above standing order on my behalf as soon as possible, to ensure that the first transfer payment is paid on time.

Sign _____ Date _____

Print Name _____

Other Services

The author also offers a portfolio building service to clients of all sizes. He will help with:

■ Sourcing the right properties tailored to your own strategy

■ Raising the cheapest finance to purchase the properties

■ Finding the right tenants

■ The ongoing maintenance of the properties.

If you are thinking of building a portfolio or need help expanding your portfolio then contact:

Ajay Ahuja BSc ACA
Accountants Direct
99 Moreton Road
Ongar
Essex
CM5 0AR

Tel: 0800 652 3979
Fax: 01277 362563
Email: emergencyaccountants@yahoo.co.uk
Web: www.accdirect.co.uk

Index of Property Hotspots